MICHAEL HONE'S

HOMOSEXUALITY

The True Lives of theFabulous Men who Preferred Men

Volume One

THE ANCIENT GREEKS

© 2014

Other books by Michael Hone: TROY; Port Beausoleil; Astorre Manfredi, The most Beautiful Boy of the Italian Renaissance; Hadrian and Antinous, Their Lives and Times; and ALCIBIADES – His Role in Athens, Sparta, Persia and Greek Love
(In French: Super Paradis)

TABLE OF CONTENTS

INTRODUCTION

The decision to write this book has its origin in a recent law in France, where I live, allowing gay marriage. Personally, I'm too young to marry and—perhaps due to my living here—I'm fully in favor of something Molière wrote, ''*Tout le plaisir de l'amour est dans le changement*,'' a quote that doesn't translate well into English and, anyway, you get the gist. So the law doesn't affect me for the moment, but it was an incredible morale booster. Legally, I was suddenly worth any other guy in this wonderful land. I came down to earth pretty fast, though, due to the riots the law occasioned. And then there are the rednecks on the quay where I have my boat (and where I'm writing this) who thought they and their sons were in dire danger the moment I ceased concealing my sexual orientation. I've never cared anything at all for American Marvel-Comics style superheroes for the simple reason that the world has been chockfull of real live heroes since recorded history. The Battles of Thermopylae and Marathon (*all* the heroes of which, as we'll soon see, preferred man-to-man/boy friendships), the exploits of Richard Coeur de Lion and Alexander the Great (both wonderfully valiant men who chanced to prefer men too), as well as innumerous other men of courage, daring and genius—are all infinitely more stirring than invented dudes who wear idiotic costumes and dodge bullets than never ever attain them. Of course, men don't have to be gay to be genial. Nothing stirs me more than the music of Mahler and guys who BASE jump off cliffs, and when Travas Pastrano did a double back flip on his motorcycle I bawled like a baby. But physically there is little resemblance between today's film heroes to the sleek, physically perfect Greeks who spent the best part of their time (when not talking philosophy and governing the city-state) keeping their bodies toned, or Renaissance lads in skintight leotards, their flies erotically molded in the form of what lies beneath, or drop fronts—cloth attached by ribbons that, when pulled, would free a man's loins when he wished to ... well, do what men just naturally do. In other words, nothing has been invented that can excel reality. And it's in the heart of that reality that I wish to begin.

The original title of this work was *HOMOSEXUALITY – the True Lives of Men who preferred Men - A Proud Heritage - A Heritage to be Proud of -*

Vol. One – Ancient Greece. **Perhaps a bit long, but the idea was—and is—to retrace the lives of Greece's most valiant gay men. Gay in the sense that their sexual preference was men, that it was with men that they fulfilled themselves intellectually and physically, men with whom they socialized, with whom they trained, did athletics, sweated in the hot baths, philosophized with in the agora or the Academy or the Lyceum. These were truly valiant men who fought and often lost their lives at Marathon, Aegospotami, Salamis, the Thermopylae and literally hundreds of other sites. Finding Greek heroes who would forward the cause of man-to-man relations was indeed easy because the counter part, gay cowards, were extremely rare among the Greeks. Volume Two--of a series that I hope will find its finality in the Renaissance--will concern Rome and already I know I'm going to have a real problem. The Greeks were men; the Romans were men too, but there were often monsters or miscreants. I'm certainly not going to write about Nero or Caligula who had a plethora of boyfriends but little or nothing of worth to write about. And what to say about the gorgeous emperor Elagabalus, assassinated at age 18, married to the charioteer Hieracles (among others) about whom he said, ''I am delighted to be called the mistress, the wife, the queen of Hieracles?'' What to say? Nothing. But we did have Trajan and Hadrian, both warriors and serious architects, both who prided themselves on leaving their wives as virgin as the day they'd found them, both of whom may really have died as virgin— heterosexually speaking—as their spouses.**

CHAPTER ONE

APOLLO – PATRON SAINT OF BOYS

The gods, the Olympians, were the first to try out boy-love. I hope that those of you who think Zeus and company have no place in a historical work will bare with me. After all, countless thousands of Greeks and Romans believed in them to such an extent that those who didn't were put to death. The believers counted among the world's most prominent thinkers, Plato, Xenophon, Pericles, Augustus, Euripides and endless others—the Athenians even hated Socrates for his hubris because he believed in the gods so strongly that he maintained he was the gods' own messenger! Today many people believe in the Holy Trinity—in other words *gods* in the plural, less numerous than the Olympians, perhaps, but still a bit crowded. Others believe in the one god, a phenomenon having its roots in Egyptology with the tenets attributed to Ikhnaton. In America 90% of the population believes in god (although only 9% says religion is the most important factor in their lives). Of this 90%, there are some extremely high-powered intellectuals. What I'm getting at is this: Who's to say what's

true or not, what exists or not? Before Schliemann no one wanted to believe in the existence of Troy, as they don't today concerning King Arthur of the Round-Table fame. So until someone comes back from the Great Beyond to give us the nitty-gritty, I'm going on with this chapter. However ... whereas I'll be as precise and exacting as possible when recounting the lives and loves of the Greeks who have helped shape our world into the wonder it is today, men who just happened to desire other men (and, for the ancients, boys), I'll allow myself a great deal of poetic license concerning those men and boys who flourished in the mists of time--the gods and their beloveds-- and the ancient heroes who existed alongside them.

By way of introducing the actors who will take part in this chapter, try to imagine dying and then awaking--as did Phoenix, the great Achilles' tutor, and Calchas, the high priest of Troy--in the presence of the Olympians themselves, as recounted by the poet:

"May I cut in a moment?" began Apollo. "Eos has told me that..." But he was interrupted by the sound of hooves and arguing outside the palace. Thetis entered, pulling old Phoenix behind. The gods showed their profound respect for the mother of the noble Achilles.

"I'm sorry if I've come at an inopportune time," said Thetis, demurely. "I wanted you to meet Phoenix, my son's teacher. He was timid about coming." Phoenix stood quaking, frightened nearly beyond endurance to find himself face to face with the Ruling Immortals whose very existence he had even on occasion put in doubt.

"Will Phoenix sup with us?" asked Zeus of Thetis.

"It'll be an honor," answered Thetis, over the wildly dissenting shakes of Phoenix' head. "And while we're on the subject," continued Thetis graciously, "I've spoken to the Fates who have informed me that Phoenix' time is not far off. They have agreed to leave the remainder of his Destiny in your hands."

"What do you wish to do throughout eternity?" asked Zeus of Phoenix.

Phoenix, far too awed to address the Supreme Force of the Universe in person, whispered emotionally in Thetis' ear. Achilles' mother nodded her head from time to time. Finally she turned to Apollo.

"His wish is to serve as guardian over your sanctuary at Delphi." And guardian over the body of Achilles' son buried at the entrance, but this Phoenix kept to himself.

Apollo went up to the old man and placed his immortal hands on the bent shoulders. "You will have your wish, my son," promised the god, younger in years than Phoenix, but his father by right of the awesome power he exercised over earthlings. "You will have in death what you never had in life: great strength and greater foresight. When your time comes, I will turn you into a giant oak that will stand guard, forever, over my temple on the heights of Mount Parnassus. From your everlasting branches you will look upon the entire world. I will make of you a symbol of life eternal, and a marker that will guide those who worship my name to my sacred altar." Apollo leaned forward and kissed the old man on the crown of his bent head.

"Well," swallowed Zeus, "Phoenix has earned his reward. I'm glad to second Apollo's noble resolution."

"Could I beg one more favor?" asked affable Apollo. "One of my priests is still on Earth. His future, too, will be a sad one unless we decide to intervene."

"Who is that, Son?"

"It's Calchas, Father."

"That spurious fool!"

"His predictions may have been a little off-center, Father, and his poetry off-key, but he was a true interpreter of my own words."

"So be it!" bellowed Zeus, filled with good humor by his own benevolent acts. "Where is he now?"

"With my Oracle at Delphi."

"Then bring him up!" ordered Father.

In a flash, Calchas vanished from before the eyes of the amazed Pythoness and reappeared in front of the Immortals.

"Ohhhh!" he cried out. "Is this any way to treat an old man!! Ohhhhh!!! Taking me away from the presence of the Pythoness!!!!"

None of the gods said a word. They stood by patiently while the prophet calmed down. Calchas frowned at them all and waited for an explanation as to what was going on. He was certain he had been snatched away by a bunch of hoodlums envious of his oracular talents. But bit-by-bit the identity of his hosts began to sink in. The white-bearded one was Zeus, the potty one Hera, the slinky one Thetis, the armored one Athena, the angelic one Artemis, and the shining one Apollo, god of Light, who came to the old man and kissed him lovingly on his weathered cheeks. "Come my child," said the omnipotent god to the awed mortal, "rest our burdens; you're now one of us." Calchas, as Phoenix before him, bent his head and shed tears of happiness and thanks, mindful that the gods reward the good with death, the wicked with treachery, and seekers of truth with blessed toil and eternal renown.

"And Mopsus...?" wept the gray-haired seer.

"Who?" asked Zeus of Apollo.

"The boy who accompanied Calchas on his travels from Troy," said Apollo to Heavenly Father. "He's one of Teiresias' sons."

"A son by Teiresias when she was a woman, or a son when he was a man?"

"Does it matter? At any rate, you needn't fear for his future," said Apollo to Calchas. "Thanks to his father's ... or his mother's ... blood and your teachings, he will become a great seer in his own right, and will even be an important member of the *Argos* in its quest for the Golden Fleece."

"Well," sniffed Zeus, "I suggest we go to my palace for a little celebratory banquet." (1)

Now, boy-love originated with Apollo, as the poet tells us:

''Phoenix was aware that Apollo was the first god to initiate night games among boys. Apollo's favorite was Hyacinthus whom the West Wind had killed by blowing back a discus the boy had thrown, shattering his skull, in reprisal for Hyacinthus' having spurned his advances. Zeus, attracted by Apollo's wailing over the lifeless corpse, wondered how boy-love could bring on such a reaction from his son. He found out when he abducted the Trojan youth Ganymede for his bed and--to ward off the smirks--dissimulated the fact by making him his cupbearer.

Soon Man followed suit. The Spartans made boy-love a virile pursuit in which lovers became valorous warriors, preferring death to the betrayal of their loved ones. The Athenians turned boy-love into a philosophical pastime in which, thanks to Eros, the intellectual and the physical were joined to make a new, self-sufficient man. In time the Trojan Aeneas would take the custom to the city he was destined to found on the banks of the Tiber. But this would be neither the virile nor intellectual fusion of body and soul known to the Greeks, but a monstrous, degenerative debauch of painted faces, effeminate bodies and fat slavering perverts.'' (1)

Apollo himself claims the credit for bringing Zeus into the fold, as the god confides to Diomedes during the Trojan War:

Apollo descended just in time to see Diomedes make off with Aeneas' immortal chargers, the very same that Zeus had given to Tros ages before in exchange for the handsome Trojan youth Ganymedes, who now served as Eternal Father's cupbearer and bedmate. Apollo reigned in the steeds and shouted a warning to fearless Diomedes that if he meddled in the mysterious ways of the gods another time, he would be dispatched at once to the vilest depths of hated Tartarus. "You're playing with fire, Diomedes, when you interfere with us Immortals and our godly gifts to Man. Now, these horses here were given to Tros, the founder of Phrygia's legendary town, in exchange for his son, a beauty if there ever was one. You probably know that Almighty Father learned the love of boys from me. He saw the way I was carrying on with Adonis and Hyacinth. Now, Hyacinth was a Spartan lad who would put ever Helen to shame. Mountain bred and cornbread fed, rosy checked and brawnily muscled, he was fancied by the West Wind too, but Hyacinth wouldn't give him a tumble. So in revenge the

Wind caught one of Hyacinth's discuses in mid-air and flung it back, striking him on his curl-graced temple. I put up such a lament when I saw my friend lifeless that Zeus came to see what was going on. I told him about Hyacinth and Father went off to try his hand at boy-love. He wasn't long in finding Ganymedes, and he was a sure-sight smarter than me: he made the lad immortal, thereby freeing him from the ravages of old age and fatal accidents. So, hand over those horses and get back to your work of killing men, not gods." Apollo then scooped up Aeneas and made away with him to safety. (1)

Although boys can't be counted on to tell the exact truth about their first loves, Apollo claims that it was the beauty of Hyacinth that lured him into night games at the side of lads. Now, Hyacinth was a Spartan, born during the Mycenaean period, long before the law of Lycurgus came into effect, making life in Sparta more difficult. After Lycurgus, boys were raised in the women's quarters until age seven, after which they were put in barracks and formed groups called herds ruled over by an older boy known as the boy-herder, who wielded a whip. They slept on reed beds, wore red cloaks, ate a sickening broth and were taught to forage for food because there was never enough in their communal messes. From age twelve the boys were free to choose older friends with whom they formed a sexual bond, friends who taught them what they needed to know about warfare and loyalty to the Spartan state. But when Hyacinth was born--before the laws of Lycurgus--Sparta was a city much like all the others in Greece, much like Athens, where boys Hyacinth's age could get a full education, had plenty to eat, and were free to hang around perfume and oil shops, and visit the barber to have their hair cared for and, when older, their nascent beards modishly trimmed.

Apollo would at times leave the stress of giving oracles at Delphi to sprawl out in the meadows of grass and flowers next to the Spartan river Eurotas. At the time Delphi was the most important site in Greece, just after Mount Olympus itself. Delphi. In the beginning the gods freed two high-flying eagles, one from the East, the other from the West. They met on the lofty crags of a great mountain that loomed over a jagged valley and the far-off port of Cirrha. Here was the sacred center of the universe; here was the spiritual navel of the Hellens; here was Delphi, home of Apollo.

For Apollo had left his birthplace on Cycladic Delos to teach Man wisdom by revealing to him the future. Apollo traveled to the heights of Mount Parnassus where he destroyed the snake-like dragon, Python, its guardian. Then, with the help of the Muses and the consent of Mother Earth, he recruited sailors from a passing Cretan ship whom he made priests, and irreproachable villagers from the nearby village of Krissa whom he ordained priestesses, sometimes called Pythonesses in memory of the dragon. He built a temple, initiated the love of the arts, taught moderation and humaneness in all things, and himself tried to exemplify the virtuous life.

But as any lad knows, at times a boy needs more than moderation and virtue. At times he wants to let out all the stops. That's why Apollo chose the meadows around Eurotas. He loved clear streams and to bask in the sun and watch the Spartan boys, naked as the day, come down to swim and horse around. It made Apollo smile to see lads as frisky as yearlings, without a care in the world, while he had to continually divvy up oracles about which king was legitimate and which was not, which state would win a war if it crossed a certain river; and what the future held in store for this lass and her beau, or for that king and his kingdom, not to mention his obligation to adjudicate over poisonings, incests, murders and crucifixions. In a sense, the least of his worries was the wear and tear between his dad Zeus and ma Hera, and brothers and sisters always and ever quarrelling.

The boy the others called Hyacinth was clearly better looking than the rest and better built, so unlike Apollo who was a bit hunky around the waist and whose buttocks were a shade large for a man. Hyacinth's were small, round and looked as solid as white marble. Of course, the sun, Apollo's brother Helios, had shaded the boy a tawny brown. The lad had long hair like Apollo, although the lad's fell over his shoulders, while Apollo's was sort of bunched up in a bun over his neck. They met when Hyacinth went to retrieve a discus he and his friends were throwing back and forth. Hyacinth was surprised to nearly stumble over Apollo, hidden in the high grass, but the god of Light had a nice warm smile and an easy way he'd learned over centuries on Earth, being Immortal and all. They fell into conversation and when his friends went home for dinner Hyacinth preferred to remain and talk with this man whose knowledge was greater than anyone the boy had ever known. Hyacinth soon left because he too was hungry but he returned day after day, his quest for knowledge insatiable. Apollo told stories about kingdoms the boy had never even heard of, and tales about kings and queens and battles and great warriors. They did physical exercises together and soon Apollo was in better shape than at any time in his life.

Lying with boys was normal intimacy for Hyacinth as the girls in Sparta were forced to remain locked up in their parent's homes and boys just naturally fell to giving each other a hand, and other things in preparation for later marriages. But this was kid stuff, just a little more physical than when giggly girls got together to spend a night at the house of one of their families. Like all the boys, Hyacinth had been raised by women, so he appreciated many of the things they liked, one of which was men. Unknown to Athenian and Spartan men was a technique practiced by all mothers—a secret passed from woman to woman, from generation to generation—a way of soothing babies and small boys by either pressing their heads against their breasts, calming them instantly thanks to the heartbeats they remembered from within the comfort of the womb, or by taking their tiny genitals in their mouths, the warmth of which had the same quieting affect.

Hyacinth was especially attracted to Apollo because the god seemed to combine both sexes. His hips nearly resembled those of women and his breasts were much fuller than a Spartan boy's. In Sparta the lads were all slim-waisted and their pectorals were squared off and as hard as a rock. So what happened was more of a surprise to Apollo than to the boy. They had met and now they loved, a new kind of experience for the otherwise very experienced god. In Greek and later Roman love, the man was always the penetrator. That much was clear. But Apollo being Apollo, the swordsman may have been, exceptionally, the young Hyacinth. At any rate, the god of Light was thrilled. Here was someone he could train with, run with, talk with, laugh with, a boy who introduced him to his friends, an intimacy that remained a closed intimacy between the two of them, but was hugely enlarged into a social event in which Apollo, Hyacinth and their friends were soon all laughing and playing and swimming and exchanging stories and knowledge. And Apollo loved the boys' laughter, so free and uninhibited and carefree and unbridled. While he and Hyacinth gave their youthful bodies in uncomplicated love, around them, hidden in the folds of grass, the other boys did the same, in pairs and in groups. Unrestrained, unruly, totally gratuitous, the end being a liberation of the demanding forces their bodies imposed on them since puberty, and then a race to the river to wash off. Hyacinth never pressured Apollo for something in exchange for the pleasure Apollo accorded him, because their release was mutual and thoroughly fulfilling and totally disinterested. Nor did the boy ever just lie there waiting for something to happen; theirs were two active virilities with never a second of monotony or boredom, something the god had not experienced with a mortal girl.

And then Apollo lost what was the most precious being to ever grace his long, long existence. Apollo had been used to inflicting pain, as the time he'd skinned alive the mortal Marsyas when in a musical contest the poor earthling--claiming to be the better musician--was outsmarted by Apollo who could play his lyre rightside-up or upside-down, while Marsyas could only make music through one end of his flute. Apollo and his fellow gods were used to raising those around them to incredible heights, before destroying them utterly, as they did Croesus, making him rich and powerful beyond dreams. Then he lost his empire to Cyrus, his precious son was gored by a boar, and his wife, when she learned of her boy's end, took her own life. Now it was the god's turn to suffer.

He and his precious beloved had spent the morning mountain climbing, they'd swum and exercised, and were now throwing the discus, their bodies, Ovid tells us, were naked and sleek with oil, while their friends, stretched out in the high grass, were chatting as boys do, and applauding the god and the youth. Now, the West Wind had been spying on the couple and had decided that he too would try his hand at boy-love. But when Hyacinth paid him no attention, he became insanely jealous and caused the discus, thrown by Apollo, to fall to the ground where it rebounded and struck the forehead of the sweet youth. Hyacinth fell and where his blood fecundated the earth a bed of hyacinth, rose-red flowers, sprang up. Apollo wailed the loss of his beloved, arousing Zeus from his noonday sleep. He saw the beauty of the boy entwined in Apollo's arms, as the god of Light shed tears that marked the flowers with spots of white, and like a flower too the boy's head hung lifeless as though cut off at the stem. Thusly were Zeus' eyes opened to the wonder of the love of boys. He immediately took a wise decision: he too would find a companion to wile away his days in mutual contentment, his nights in shared bliss, but as a first step, he would make the lad immortal.

Apollo had put all his science into reviving Hyacinth's still-warm body but its life had flitted away and already Hades had risen from the Underworld to claim what was his. Apollo stopped him with a glance, and womanish or not, Hades knew the look in those eyes and trembled, for he was confronted with the god of Light himself, who, next to Hermes, was Zeus' favorite son. So he crept back into the caverns of molten slime that awaited him. Apollo gently picked up the boy and carried him to the Elysian Fields, meadows and islands untouched by sorrow, a blessed land, the home of heroes and the deathless gods, a land free from toil, cradle of perpetual springs and shady groves and bubbling brooks, a cornucopia warmed by its own sun and illumined by its own stars--and eternally cooled by the West Wind, an obligation demanded by Apollo under pain of death.

And there Hyacinth lives, in Elysium, and in us, for the blood he shed nourished the sweet earth, the sweet earth that nourishes us so abundantly to this very day.

CHAPTER TWO

LAIUS – MANKIND'S FIRST BOY LOVER
ORESTES AND PYLADES

If Apollo was the first god to play at night games with boys, the first man was Laius. From Sophocles' trilogy we learn that the baby Oedipus is handed over to a servant to be killed in order to prevent the accomplishment of an oracle, an oracle stating that he will kill his father and marry his mother. He does both after solving the riddle of the sphinx (which creature becomes four-footed, then two-footed and finally three-footed?). His mother, when she finds out she's been enjoying her own son, commits suicide and Oedipus blinds himself when he discovers that he's killed his father and slept with his mother. In *Oedipus at Colonus* Oedipus dies and we learn more about his children Antigone, Polyneices and Eteocles. In *Antigone* Polyneices is accused of treason and killed. His body is thrown outside the city walls and the king forbids its burial, under pain of death. Antigone does so anyway and, faced with death, she commits suicide, followed by the king's son who was going to wed her, followed by the king's wife who couldn't face losing her precious son. (2)

This family's ups and downs began with Laius, son of the Theban king Labdacus. His father was killed in war and Laius, too young to reign, was forced to flee. He was welcomed by Pelops, king of Pisa, near Mycenae, and raised with Pelops' son Chrysippus, a boy younger than Laius, whom Laius taught to become a master charioteer, winning a race in the Nemean Games. As Laius had lost his father and as Pelops was known to be harsh with his son Chrysippus, the man and the boy gravitated toward one another, compensating for what was lacking in the other, founding what was to become the paradigm for all later Greek societies, from Sparta to Athens to Crete: that a man will take to himself a boy whom he'll teach to be virtuous by instilling in him knowledge, by training his body and by preparing him for the life of a warrior, initiating him into the ways of men, which are the ways of the world. Laius returned to Thebes with Chrysippus and recaptured his father's throne. As expected of him, he took a wife whom he was not expected to bed as the Oracle at Delphi predicted that should he do so he'd sire his own murderer. He kept on, therefore, with Chrysippus until his father Pelops' wife, Hippodamia, Chrysippus' stepmother, came to Thebes to be reunited with her stepson. No one suspected that the real reason for her sudden appearance was that she and her rightful sons, Atreus and Thyestes, had been cast out of Mycenae, and Pelops now prepared to name Chrysippus as his heir. She thusly had her sons sneak into Laius and Chrysippus' bedroom where they lay entwined. Atreus plunged a dagger into Chrysippus heart, Thyestes another into his neck.

At the loss of his beloved, Laius drank himself into an inconsolable drunken stupor during which he consummates his marriage with his wife, who brings forth Oedipus. The boy is ordered slain by Laius (because of the Oracle's prediction that he'll kill his father) but he escapes death, only to return home as a young man. He came upon his father, whom he didn't recognize, at a crossroads and was ordered to give way so that Laius could pass. When he refused to do so, Laius lashed him with his whip and ordered his chariot forward, the wheel of which rolled over the boy's foot (from whence comes the word Oedipus, meaning swollen foot). Oedipus grabbed hold of Laius' whip, causing him to fall to the ground. Furious with anger, the boy took out his dagger, grabbed the head by the hair that he held firmly against his thigh, while he slit open the throat from ear to ear.

The origin of this incredible mayhem began with the sin of the father, as does all mayhem. In this case Pelops, as a young man himself, ventured into the kingdom of a certain Oenomaus who possessed immense wealth and had a wondrous daughter, Hippodamia. Oenomaus proclaimed that any boy could have her for wife, as long as he won a chariot race against the king himself. A dozen lads had already tried, their head at present adorned the castle walls. Pelops decided he would not be the thirteenth. He bribed the man who cared for the king's chariot, Myrtilus, by offering him half of Oenomaus kingdom and the right to sleep with Hippodamia, the first to force her virginal hymen. The offer inspired Myrtilus to replace the king's chariot axle with linchpins made of wax, thusly provoking his death when the axle broke and the king's body was reduced to a pulp as it was dragged behind his horses. Pelops then accompanied Myrtilus to the top of a cliff in order for them both to survey the kingdom they now shared, and pushed him over. At the bottom of the cliff Myrtilus lived long enough to curse Pelops and his descendants, Chrysippus, the son he preferred, as well as his boys Atreus and Thyestes.

Pelops sent his sons to Mycenae to be co-kings, but Atreus out manipulated Thyestes and took over the kingship himself. Thyestes got his revenge by sleeping with Atreus' wife. When Atreus found out, he invited Thyestes to a dinner of reconciliation. Atreus met his long-absent brother Thyestes with crocodile tears and endearments. Thyestes for his part was moved by the display of affection and the summons bringing him back from exile to share the throne with his ruling brother.

Graciously Atreus led Thyestes to a waiting bath where he was refreshed and oiled, and then to the resplendent table where they dined on tender exotic meats from a sculptured cauldron. The time passed in friendly conversation. Finally, when the rules of hospitality had been observed, Thyestes requested that his sons be brought before him in order that he might share the joy of his return and announce Atreus' decision to install him, again, as co-king of Mycenae.

Atreus at once gave the order to bring forth the boys. A servant brought a huge platter of inlaid silver that he set on the dining table. He removed the lid.

Thyestes stared uncomprehendingly into shiny crimson forms attached pell-mell by a viscous substance not unlike a deep-scarlet gel. Slowly before his unbelieving eyes the forms took shape, the darker ones matted hair, the pale ones curves of bluish skin, the shiny ones nails and teeth, the glassy ones half-opened eyes; and finally the immediate recognition: the five heads and ten hands of his sons.

"And the bodies," said Atreus, "are within their father's stomach."

Thyestes rose up--overturning the table and its contents in his haste--and seized by heaving spasms, bent over and vomited onto the squalid debris.

But before evading his own slaughter at the hands of his brother, and making his escape, he put a curse on all the descendants of the house of Atreus, from whose seed was to come Agamemnon and Menelaus; while from the loins of Thyestes issued Aegisthus, his avenger. (1)

Menelaus, king of Sparta, couldn't prevent Paris from seducing his wife Helen, and spent ten years fighting over her at the foot of the walls of mighty Troy. They both eventually returned to Sparta to die in the anonymity of that strange—and thoroughly unique—land. Agamemnon, king of Mycenae, returned home with Cassandra, a cold virgin that he had somehow brought to life after the collapse of Troy and the death of her parents. Agamemnon's wife Clytemnestra and her lover, Thyestes' son Aegisthus, awaited their arrival.

Clytemnestra and Aegisthus stood on the ramparts of Mycenae. In the distance an incursion of the sea shone silver in the morning's first light. On the steep, well-trodden dirt road leading up from the shore to the mountain citadel they spotted a small whirlwind of dust. It belonged to Agamemnon and his retinue who were approaching. Clytemnestra took hold of Aegisthus' arm and looked up at him. Never had she seemed so small and frail; never had her eyes spoken with such clarity to his. Had a passer-by not been aware of what had preceded their dawn meeting on the city's walls, he would have assumed the queen clutched to her lover out of fear in the face of Agamemnon's impeding arrival, and the adultery he would inevitably discover. But Aegisthus knew the look. She was thanking him for the night he had given her: if Clytemnestra was no longer a crone, it was due to the young man at her side. Aegisthus put an arm around her waist and took her hand in his own. He was two decades younger than the queen whose corpulence betrayed her inexorable decline. His natural preference was towards young girls, yet the woman he now held offered the emotional tranquility that an infancy of betrayal and death had deprived him. No one and nothing could replace the warm assurance of the never-changing hollow alongside Clytemnestra's thigh that was his refuge in their sturdy bed. Nor could anything take the place of the haven between her breasts where his head lay sheltered from demented dreams, lulled to sleep by the regular, reassuring beats of her heart.

"Are you worried?" he asked.

"Only about losing you."

"I've had the palace surrounded. The storm destroyed most of his ships and men. Only he and a few others got through. They pose no threat. Agamemnon has been restored to his own country and it is here amidst his people, our ancestors and the laws that govern all men that he must be judged. There is nothing more terrible than the verdict demanded by the native soil. A man can delude himself but not the earth from which he emerged. The earth knows the reason for our every act, and forces us to account for our every crime. It is unforgetting and unforgiving; unlike one's conscience, it cannot be salved."

"Yet it is we--not the earth or the spirits who dwell within it--who will do the judging."

"I only hope he has returned with much gold," she said looking down. "It will be needed for his death mask."

Agamemnon and Cassandra sped along the dirt road that crossed the flat Argos Valley before winding its way up the slope leading to the citadel. A thin blanket of powdered snow incompletely covered rocky outcroppings, stunted undergrowth and the pale-gray soil. Both the king and his mistress were wrapped in sheepskins.

"Can you see me camping beside the ship when my city is but a few leagues away? We'll be home in an hour," Agamemnon was saying.

"Please wait for the other ships to come in." Visions, as yet incomprehensible, fought to surface in Cassandra's mind. They filled her with foreboding, warning her that both she and Agamemnon were in peril. "You haven't been to Mycenae in a decade. How do you know what's awaiting you? Clytemnestra may have come to thirst for the power she inherited when you left; her welcome may not be as you imagine. And then ... the news that she has a consort."

"The queen has no consort! In the name of Zeus, Cassandra, believe that as her husband I know from firsthand experience she no longer felt the need of our being together as man and wife. There are certain flames that cannot be stoked once they're dead."

"Before you," she smiled, "one could have said the same for me." It had indeed taken the cataclysm to breach the emptiness between Cassandra's inner void and the fullness known as life.

"All I did was bring you back from a long sleep. Your gratitude for my saving your life opened the gates of trust that you had closed against all those who refused to have faith in you."

"That's what you are doing now, my king, refusing to have faith in me. If your confidence in me were total, you would turn back."

"Your fears are groundless."

"I'm so close to seeing," said Cassandra, "but there's still a veil before my eyes. Until it's raised, premonitions guide me. I feel the evil within the city; Mycenae is enveloped in the shadow of doom."

"Even if Clytemnestra were planning to keep the regency, how could she? I've got the army."

"What's left of it. In the intervening years Mycenaean boys too young to go off to Troy have grown to manhood. Mycenae's real army is inside her walls. Those who return from Phrygia with you are old, crippled and exhausted."

"If the gates are closed and the ramparts armed, we'll turn back. I'll wait for the other ships and then go to Menelaus in Sparta to replenish our troops. Spartans wouldn't revolt against their state; they, at least, have the needed respect for their leaders."

"What will you tell her?"

"That her place has been taken by another. I will let her run the palace; you will be free to be with me."

"And the children?"

"Orestes and Electra will remain with us. But our own progeny will rule after we're gone."

"It sounds so perfect. Could the queen have already learned about us?"

''I suppose some of the deserters could have brought back word. That we'll know very soon."

The king brought his chariot to a stop at the entrance to the citadel, the Lion Gate, a portal of cyclopean stones surmounted by a pair of felines facing each other like two enemies frozen in the attitudes of arrogance and mistrust. He stepped down with Cassandra at his side. The gate, the Great Way beyond, and the palace atop of the hill, seemed somehow familiar to her. She looked about in bewilderment. The walls were lined with Mycenaeans, none of whom doubted that she was as hopelessly mad as she had been depicted, time and again, in the stories they had heard over the past ten years. They stared at her and Agamemnon in silence. Was this old man really their chief, the warrior whom most of them were too young to remember? Was it he who had left for Troy carrying the scepter that gave him rule over Mycenae? Was this decrepit wreck he who was now the acknowledged sovereign of Greece and Asia?

Agamemnon wondered if the silence was the awe in which his people held him. He was used to polite respect, but their motionless acclaim was troubling. He made certain his bodyguard surrounded him, and then ascended the Great Way that climbed steeply to the top of the hill. He glanced up to his palace and saw Clytemnestra watching from the top of the ramparts. A wind, barely felt where he was but fierce at the summit, made her dress flap wildly behind while adhering in the front, giving the impression she was naked. He was reminded of one of the statues of the Winged Victory he had seen during his voyages, an inauspicious coincidence, he thought, given the circumstances. The king also saw Aegisthus, but dismissed him as one of the ubiquitous servants.

Clytemnestra left the walls and went to meet him in the center of the small courtyard in front of the palace. The courtyard was surrounded by a low wall with a small wooden gate. It was at the gate that Agamemnon bid Cassandra wait, fearful that she would be badly received by his wife who may have heard of their union. There were but five steps between him and the queen, and in taking them he bridged a decade.

"I know how men in foreign lands dream of home," were his first words. He saw the lines that marked her face; he wondered how many times she had struggled to put on the dresses of her youth before settling into middle age. It was his stubby beard with the white hairs and his chalky, blue-veined cheeks and furrowed throat she first saw. He was a wizened shadow of his former regal authority, although the rigors of war had not been able to keep a paunch from forming. Her superiority over him made her smile. Agamemnon waited for words of welcome.

Behind Clytemnestra, out of the dark doorway that led into the palace, came Orestes, discretely but firmly pushed forward by Electra. Agamemnon guessed at once who he must be.

"Even more comforting than the first glimpse of land to a storm-tossed sailor is the sight of one's own son," said the king, intent on making his first words and actions memorable. He went to Orestes and took the child in his arms. Never before had anyone seen tears in Agamemnon's eyes.

"Here's your welcome," said Clytemnestra, still smiling, her hands gently resting on Orestes' shoulders.

"Electra, my daughter," he said, embracing the girl at Orestes' side. "I've brought back Cassandra from Troy. Will you help me look after her? She's your age. With her assistance I'll be better able to govern Phrygia, our new colony."

He turned to Clytemnestra and gave her orders to care for his personal guard and send slaves to unload his boat. They were to be closely supervised because of the gold he had returned with. His tone was already brisk and impersonal. The once familiar taste of being trampled under, that Clytemnestra had been spared during the last years, came to her mouth. If her plan were not other, she would have defiled him then and there with the bile that rose in her throat. "I will see to it myself," she murmured. "We've been expecting you for a long time--several months already. Your rooms are in order." She made a sign to a servant to bring the king a cup of wine that Clytemnestra had herself prepared.

"Your bath is waiting. I'll have a tub brought to the guest room for Cassandra."

"I can go a little longer without being oiled and massaged. Ten years of hardships have made your civilized ways superfluous. If you can't tolerate the smell of me, go to the women's quarters. Anyway, I have important work to do. I can't let Greece and Asia slip through my fingers now that I hold them so solidly."

"Can't Greece and Asia be put aside until you've rested? There are delegations that wish to see you, but before there are things which must be explained."

Secrets for my ears alone, smirked Agamemnon. She's had power for a long time. It will be difficult for her to give it up. Of course, I could strip her of prestige with a snap of my fingers, as I could snap her neck, but to what purpose? She might still be useful. After all, she has kept the country in one piece since I left. She deserves some priority to my influence.

"I suppose a bath won't do any harm and I suddenly feel weary ... wearier than I had thought. All at once the weight of all these years ... has made me exhausted," he said, handing the emptied cup back to the servant.

"May I take your sword for you, sire?" asked Aegisthus who had been standing among a small group of servants next to the queen. Agamemnon failed to notice with what deference the others held the young man who so kindly volunteered as his valet.

"Let him take it, husband. Enter the house unarmed. Let it be a new beginning."

"Yes," agreed Agamemnon, handing over the weapon. "Here I will reign in peace."

"Let us enter, husband."

"Please, take care of Cassandra," he repeated as he advanced towards the black doorway. "She isn't a slave, you know, anymore than Apollo and Poseidon were slaves when they were forced to build Troy's walls."

"I'll have my personal servant, Crobyle, attend to her," said Clytemnestra, nodding to the girl to go to Cassandra.

"We will show her what a gracious people we are," continued Agamemnon.

Welcome home, husband, thought Clytemnestra. Welcome to the house that has been my prison since your murderous sword destroyed my husband Tantalus, and brought me here as much your booty and your whore as Cassandra.

Welcome home, son of the assassin, thought Aegisthus. Welcome to the place where your father deprived mine of his rightful throne.

"Give her the free use of all the apartments. Even in her own city she had been caged like an animal," said the king.

Come inside, thought Clytemnestra, as they neared the ominous entrance. She gripped Agamemnon's arm tightly as if afraid he would turn and bolt at the last moment.

Enter old man, thought Aegisthus. Thyestes and my brothers have poured your bath. Enter its tenebrous waters: they will draw you down to the abysmal depths of Hades.

"I'll take her for walks through the olive groves. Like a young kitten her faith will have to be won little by little," said Agamemnon, as he crossed the shadowy threshold and disappeared into the yawning chasm.

Here I am, father, thought Aegisthus, following the king in. And this is what I've become. Have I made you proud? And he too vanished through the gaping hole.

From within came silence, while those outside waited motionless and fearful as though an unseen power held them suspended. Cassandra knelt at the gatepost. Few were close enough to hear her words. Only the servant Crobyle bent beside the trembling figure that was madly gripping the post, her body wracked by the images emerging in her mind.

"The blood," she moaned as Crobyle leaned cautiously forward to catch her mutterings. "The blood. The blood is everywhere." Her wild, obsessed eyes filled Crobyle with fear. She wondered at how the king could have returned from foreign lands with such a creature for his slave. She made a movement to back away when Cassandra deliriously seized her hands and pressed them against her feverish forehead. For a moment the Trojan princes, her mouth agape, listened to the lines etched in Crobyle's palms. Then she looked into the servant's eyes. "The boy," she whispered. "You have to save the boy. He mustn't be soiled by the blood. Take him away NOW!" A chill of terror shook Crobyle. Cassandra thrust Crobyle's hands between her breasts, pulling Crobyle within an inch of herself. Crobyle was hypnotized by the insane eyes, dead and alive like scorching blue ice. "They're all gone," whimpered the princess in a low, guttural moan. "Brothers and sisters, Priam and Hecabe, Andromache and Hector, even the children, all gone, just dogs and vultures left. And I saw it all. I saw them die when Paris first came within our walls. I suffered their deaths again when Hector went through the gates to meet Achilles, and still again when Trojans accepted the Greeks' parting gift. Why haven't the images rendered me mad? Must I see my loved ones die time and time again until my own head falls on this very spot, staining the ash-gray earth? And even then will I know peace? But enough of me; my fate has long since been sealed. It is within the palace that the Destiny of what remains of the Greek people is unfolding. The curse that has wrought ruin on this house is coming to an end, and a Mycenaean tomb will soon close on its last king. Without its leaders Greece will be unable to turn back the mountain peoples at her borders. When the barbarians enter, a millennium of fear and ignorance will descend upon the Earth. That is the price the Fates have exacted to carry through Thyestes' curse.

"Yet a survivor could delay the inevitable," continued Cassandra. "Orestes is innocent of bloodguilt. For him to remain within this house will mean his death: Aegisthus will kill him for the man he will one day become. Orestes is the last heir. With him dead, there can be no survival for his people. But should his life be spared, there will be a gleam of hope for still unborn generations. Go to him, Crobyle. Save his eyes from the visions that corrupted the heart of Aegisthus. Flee with him, and remain by his side."

The servant, whose pure heart was as guileless as a child's, never doubted for a moment the beseeching words. She left Cassandra leaning against the open wooden gate, and ran across the courtyard into the palace to shield Orestes from the rabid horrors so clearly reflected in Cassandra's eyes.

Cassandra remained alone, her head bent, staring into the gray earth over which the acts taking place within the palace played as on a mirror. Agamemnon was stepping out of the shallow basin where he had been bathed, onto the royal carpet that Clytemnestra had laid for him. The queen advanced with a garment to cover her husband's nakedness. Made by herself, it was a tunic of knotted netting as fine as a web and as solid as strands of bronze. Agamemnon was eyeing the nearby banquet table full of the delicacies war had deprived him for so many years. A servant girl guessed his wish and brought him a blood-red apple that he bit into. Clytemnestra came forward with the garment that had neither holes for the head nor the arms. The king bent to permit her to slip it over. And it was there, neither on dry land nor in water, neither dressed nor naked, neither eating nor fasting, that the trap was sprung. Agamemnon, firmly ensnared in the net, saw Aegisthus race forward with the king's own sword stretched high above his head. It hovered but a moment before falling with all the force of twenty years of revengeful rage. So rapid were the events that neither the blur of the oncoming Aegisthus, nor the screams from Cassandra outside, served to warn Agamemnon that his precious life had drawn to an end. The king toppled backwards into the crimson pool, his severed head trapped by the net against his chest, the trunk spewing out its crimson essence, each spurt in cadence to the faltering heart, each less valiant than the preceding. The blood was indeed everywhere.

At the same moment a signal was given for the palace guards to go to the barracks near the Lion Gate and massacre those who had returned from Troy with Agamemnon. And Clytemnestra, in a rabid frenzy, went to Aegisthus and seized her husband's sword. In her delirious hand it weighed no more than the royal scepter.

Outside, Cassandra saw the queen racing through the throne room, yet even then--with her own annihilation but moments away--the maddening images gave no relent: In her mind's eye she saw the fall of the house of Atreus. She saw Crobyle and Orestes, both wrapped in disguising rags, make their way down the tree-bare, snow-carpeted pass which took them from the Mycenaean citadel to the Argos Road. From there they went north, to King Strophius' court at the foot of craggy Mount Parnassus where he would be raised with Pylades, Strophius' son, and soon Orestes' beloved. For seven years Orestes would be nurtured on stories of honor and hate, and grow up knowing that to avenge was his fate. He learned how his father was slain, and that only through his mother's death, and that of her consort, would he remove the stain from the house of Atreus and regain his rightful throne. Upon reaching manhood Orested and his inseparable lover returned to the land from whence Orestes came, and there, in front of the tomb of his father, Orestes showed Agamemnon the man he had become. He knelt before the beehive's sealed doors and offered a sprig of his hazel hair. Lost in thought, he and Pylades did not hear Electra approach through dawn's wintry mist until she stood above them, tall, stern and gaunt from the years of cancerous wrath. Brother and sister fell into each other's arms, and only the gentle prodding of his friend made them give up the remembrances of the past, and carry out the plan the two boys had formulated and rehearsed a thousand times together at Strophius' court.

Cassandra saw Electra rush off to the palace where she found Clytemnestra unnerved by another of her delirious dreams, this one concerning a serpent that had sucked blood from the queen's breast. The serpent was Orestes, clamored the queen, Orestes who would return to draw blood from his own mother as surely as the serpent had suckled its fill. How surprised was she, then, when Electra informed her that an oxcart was climbing the Great Way with the ashes of Orestes, dead from the sweating sickness. The queen sent Electra to find Aegisthus, overjoyed by the news. He came into the palace unarmed, for with Orestes dead he no longer feared being harmed. The three--usurper, murderess and offended-- waited by the throne-room door. Finally Pylades entered with the golden urn, following by hooded Orestes, armed with Agamemnon's uncleansed sword that Electra had hidden for him. The queen and her king marveled over the sealed vessel, while Orestes from behind struck off--with a single sweep--the heads of his foe. Orestes, too, had passed the final, age-old test; and outside, in his murky tomb, Agamemnon found eternal rest.

The images ceased.

Cassandra's own head rolled across the sun-lit courtyard, and Clytaernnestra, sword in hand, addressed the horrified crowd: "Return to your homes. I have taken the fate of the city in my hands: the evil that has threatened our survival has been purged. A death has demanded a death, a betrayal a betrayal, an injustice an injustice. The curse of Thyestes on the house of Atreus is at an end. It has run its course: like a forest fire--wild and relentless--it has indiscriminately destroyed generation after generation until coming at last to the immutable calm of a lake's edge. We will now know that calm; the chain of events is over; order has been established. We have yielded to circumstance, and from the ashes of our misery will spring a new and better season. Go to your hearths; your queen has cast out the malediction." (1)

About Orestes and Pylades the famous rhetorician Lucian wrote, ''Invoking Eros as the mediator of their love for each other, they sailed together, as it were, in one and the same ship of life.'' Lucian goes on: ''Such love is always like that; for when from boyhood a serious love has grown up and it becomes adult at the age of reason, the long-loved object returns reciprocal affection, and it is hard to determine which is the lover of which, for--as from a mirror--the affection of the lover is reflected from the beloved.'' As Orestes and Pylades were the same age, there was, as with Alexander and Hephaestion, no clear lover and no clear beloved. Some recent observers who have studied male-to-male relations among the ancient Greeks have concluded that such a distinction may have been far less important than we've come to believe, and that, as today, some boys simply have a preference for penetrating, others for being penetrated. In other sexual acrobats, intercrural (between the thighs penetration), fellatio, et al, the distinctions vanish.

CHAPTER THREE

SON MY, AVENGER MY : AEGISTHUS
THE WORLD'S FIRST BOY-LOVE EVANGELIST : ORPHEUS
HYLAS

An old Trojan inscription has been unearthed that relates the role of a son in his father's life. The inscription says, *Son My, Avenger My.* This was the role that Thyestes had in mind when he fled the palace of his brother Atreus, after having ingested the flesh of his sons. This was the role bequeathed to Aegisthus:

Outside the cyclopean walls of Agamemnon's fortified citadel were the numerous habitations of Mycenae's citizens, soldiers, artisans, farmers, servants and slaves. On the corner of a muddy street was a two-story wooden house of many rooms. Behind the door of one were a large unmade bed, an old wall tapestry, floor rugs and a dressing table piled with cosmetics. Corinna was seated before it putting on make-up. Aegisthus was lying on the bed. Corinna was talking.

"You've been bottled up here too long waiting for the queen's answer to your message. I'm the only sport you've had in days. If you don't get some news soon from the palace you'll turn into a mushroom."

Aegisthus sat up at the end of the bed, one leg dangling over the side, the other folded in front of him. Entirely naked, his white cloak and chiton hung from a wall peg. Although small as a boy and not broad as most Mycenaeans, he was well muscled and taller than his contemporaries. He watched Corinna apply blue paint over her eyelids. A yellow dressing gown with low-cut neckline bordered with white and red bands of ribbon hung loosely about her shoulders. With the exception of Sparta which was known for its beautiful women, Aegisthus had rarely come across a courtesan as graceful as Corinna. He studied her breasts, his hand absently fondling himself.

"You mustn't be jealous, precious," Corinna continued, eyeing him through the mirror. She turned and took his face in her uplifted palms. "While in your care I'll remain faithful to you. It's just that sometimes I have to pay visits to old friends. You wouldn't want me to stop seeing everybody, would you?" She kissed him on the forehead, leaving a red smudge that she wiped away with a piece of soft cloth. She put the cloth to her lips, wet it, and gently patted off the beads of perspiration from his creased brow and the base of his nose. "You're so hot. You really must go out for air."

"It'll be safer tonight," he answered docilely. "Maybe there's a place I can take you?"

She flicked the hair back from his shoulders and again gazed at his scar.

"No," she said distractedly, "I'm having dinner with friends, but I'll be able to join you later."

"What friends? You've said nothing about being away tonight."

"My dearest, in spite of all the love I have for you, there's one thing I can't take, and that's feeling entrapped. I'm a professional woman and as such I have to keep certain important contacts." She returned to the mirror. Through it she saw Aegisthus bite his lip. In a lighter voice she continued: "But it is *just* a dinner. Afterwards we'll be back together and spend the night in any way you wish. Do you agree, my beauty?"

A man in body but emotionally a boy stunted in adolescence, Aegisthus, too, was of the race of the fatherless. "Sure," he said, ill at ease.

It was Corinna's habit of drying the perspiration from his forehead and the slopes of his nostrils with a cloth dampened by her lips that reminded Aegisthus of his mother. He bent forward and gently opened Corinna's robe, enough to release her breasts.

His mother Pelopia, too, had painted her nipples with rouge. As a young boy he had spent hours sitting cross-legged on her bed, silently watching her come and go between her bath and wardrobe, trailing a scent of oil and perfume, as naked beneath her dressing gown as Corinna. Even when Atreus, the man he had believed to be his father, came to mount her, the boy's presence had been encouraged as a lesson in the engendering that would be his future responsibility as king.

The day of his youth he remembered most clearly was to serve as another kind of lesson. Atreus' brother Thyestes, a renegade on whose head Atreus had placed a talent of gold after a previous escape, had been captured outside the walls of Mycenae while trying to foment the population against the king. After having him thrown into prison, Atreus gave his son an incredible order, ending it with the promise, "This night will make of you a man." He was so right.

Armed with a sword entrusted by his mother for his birthday, Aegisthus snuck down the tower steps to the dungeon. He was terrified of the task he had been ordered to accomplish, but more terrified still at the thought of disobeying Atreus. Painstakingly, he unlocked the door to Thyestes' cell. The room was in darkness except for a streak of light that came through the partially-opened door and fell across the gently-heaving back turned towards him. He walked to within two feet of the inert figure. Trembling, he raised the sword above his head and in line with the uncovered neck that lay below. His veins, temples, heart and throat throbbed as he brought the great piece of iron down onto the cot, severing it in two.

He had had no time to reflect on what had happened. No sooner had he struck than he was shoved to the floor and pinned there. He lay in excruciating pain, his arms twisted over his shoulder blades, Thyestes' knee planted in the small of his back. Wordless, Thyestes grasped the sword with his free hand and applied the blade to the back of the boy's neck, producing a long band of blood.

Thyestes would have severed off the head in seconds had he not recognized the weapon. "Who gave you this?" he had asked.

"My mother," Aegisthus had cried out.

Thyestes grabbed the boy by the hair and turned his face into the light. Aegisthus felt the man's body twitch. "You're just a child!" he said. "What mother would send an infant to carry out murder?"

At those words Aegisthus had broken into tears. He told Thyestes that it had been his father, Atreus, who had sent him. The sword had been a gift to the boy from his mother, Pelopia. Thyestes now knew that his revenge would be complete. After Atreus had cut up and fed him parts of his sons, Thyestes had escaped to Delphi where he begged the Pythoness to help him in his vengeance. She instructed him to impregnate Pelopia, his own daughter, which he did wearing a mask so as not to be recognized. The Pythoness, for whom the future was an open book, knew that Atreus was destined to fall in love with Pelopia. Although Aegisthus was born early, Atreus naturally believed the boy was the fruit of his own loins.

None of this Thyestes revealed to the boy. He pulled him to his feet and applied his mantle to the cut on his neck. He told him that he would be spared if he obeyed two commands.

The first was for the boy to fetch his mother and bring her to the cell, offering for reason that there was a prisoner who knew the whereabouts of her father.

Pelopia agreed to descend to the dungeon, and to her son's amazement, she threw herself to Thyestes' feet, weeping and thanking the gods for his having been restored to her. Thyestes' reaction was to pick up the sword and ask Pelopia from whence it came. Embarrassed, she requested that Aegisthus leave the cell. When Thyestes insisted he stay, she confessed that just before her marriage to Atreus she had been defiled by a man whose face she had not seen, and who had lost the sword when a passing guard forced him to flee.

Thyestes studied the sword for many moments, remembering that dark night when, added by drink, he had raped her. Finally he looked into Pelopia's eyes and said, "It is mine."

Aegisthus did not understand the impact of the words. He did not think his mother understood either at first. But suddenly her eyes opened wide. Her body shook and from her mouth came an animal howl. Thyestes did not move; his face was empty of expression. He showed no emotion as she gripped the sharp blade that cut into her hands, and thrust it into her stomach.

It was this, the loss of his mother, before his eyes, more than the mistreatment at Atreus' hands, which produced the wounds and mutilations on the boy's soul, welts perverting the spirit as cruelly as lash marks disfiguring the body.

Corinna felt Aegisthus' grip tighten on her shoulders. She turned and saw tears in his eyes. "What is it, my beauty?" she asked, wiping them away with her fingertips, "What is it?"

He smiled to reassure her and shook his head. "The accumulation of too many things. So much has gone wrong. The time must certainly come when the Fates will favor the cause of those they have until now forsaken." Of Aegisthus Corinna knew only about the missive he had sent Queen Clyaemnestra. Not for a moment did she believe there would be an answer, and even now her mind was struggling with the problem of how she would eventually rid herself of him. She turned back to her mirror.

As his mother lay bleeding to death, Aegisthus had felt the man's hands shake him back to consciousness. "She's a traitor, boy, a traitor to her brothers and her father," he lied. "Atreus is our enemy; he is hated by our people; and she was his wife."

Thyestes extracted a dagger from Pelopia's belt, and drew out the sword from her body. It made a sucking sound; to this day and after a hundred battles, Aegisthus could not remember that sound without feeling the salt rise to his mouth and the need to vomit. Kneeling before him Thyestes said: "Aegisthus! I am your father! I am your father, Aegisthus!" Thyestes' feverish eyes left no doubt as to his veracity, and answered what the boy had secretly wished of the gods: the death of the man who had beaten him into obedience, and, like the beast Atreus was, had forced himself upon his mother, in Aegisthus' presence, again and again and again.

"The second command," Thyestes continued, "will make it possible for me to regain the throne that will one day be your legacy. Only you can approach Atreus. Take this dagger and when he is asleep, go into his bedchamber and kill him. But I warn you," he said, shaking the boy by the shoulders, "do not fail us. Our lives and our fortunes depend on you. Now be off!"

Aegisthus had crept into Atreus' rooms. The king was lying full length on his couch, his eyes closed. Aegisthus approached. Recognizing the boy's steps, the king said, "It that you, Son?" Aegisthus replied, "Do not doubt, Father," and drove the dagger into the bared throat.

Even after twenty years, the visions of the murder stunned Aegisthus into a numb stupor that the knock at the door dispelled. Corinna went to it and spoke for a few moments with an elderly woman. She returned with a message she gave to Aegisthus.

"It's from the queen," he said. "Listen: 'Your presence in Mycenae and the letter you sent me have put your life in danger. I beg of you to remain concealed. Agamemnon will soon part on a long voyage and I will be in a better position to grant you audience. Await my messenger. Keep courage.' It's not signed. Are you sure it came from the palace?"

"Yes, Crobyle just told me it was delivered by a palace servant--one especially trusted by Clytaemnestra. So, you are to be received by the queen?"

"Yes, and take back what is mine."

"The palace guard is faithful to Agamemnon."

"When he dies, they will be faithful to the new king."

"It is common talk that Clytaemnestra is pregnant. If she has a son, Mycenae will be assured an heir."

"She will have a son and his name will be Orestes. The Priest Calchas has prophesied his coming," said Aegisthus, "and the unique fate the gods have decreed be his. The son will prove as mortal as the father."

"To become king you will need the help of Clytaemnestra."

"I shall have it. Do you doubt my charm?" He rose and pulled her to him. His new luck gave him force. Staring into her eyes, he drew her hand down to his lengthening power that she grasped. She would not be leaving him this night. "It will all take time, but I shall regain what belonged to my father."

"Didn't Thyestes inherit the throne with Atreus' death?"

"Yes. He became king. But before he could raise an army he was attacked on all sides by Atreus' allies, led by Helen's father, King Tyndareus of Sparta, acting for Atreus' two sons, Agamemnon and Menelaus. Thyestes was again banished and this time he died in exile, a useless man, driven to ruin by Agamemnon. Only I have not forgotten him. Through me his ghost will see his seed rule once more over Mycenaeans. He will win his final vindication. And over his grave I shall sacrifice all kinsmen from the house of Atreus until my father in Hades gluts himself on their blood."

"You make me feel so ... queasy."

"Kiss me," he said, parting her robe. "In a while I shall have to see Clytamnestra. Your love will make it easier to face that old horse."

She shivered.

"You needn't fear me, Corinna." His voice was shallow and shaky. "I'm but Thyestes' shadow, a spirit whose only purpose is the continuation of his line. It is Destiny who has called upon me to destroy my father's enemies. Agamemnon should fear me, not you." He swung her around, her back to him, and pulled the robe from her body, while in the mirror he saw his hands cup her uplifted breasts. Before she could refuse, his hand covered her mouth to stifle her cry, while from behind he entered with a practiced thrust. He was of the size, he knew, that could placate even a queen, and rekindle her desire. As Corinna's tears ran over his fingers, he perpetrated the act practiced between boys in preparation for the girls they, as young men, left virgin until marriageable age. "No, you need not fear me, Corinna. For you I am no more than your lover. For Agamemnon I am what every son must be to his father: his avenger." (1)

The consequences of such a heinous act as the murder of a mother by her son were well within the understanding of Hera. Until Clytemnestra's assassination, Motherhood had been held in the loftiest respect. Who could guarantee the survival of the species, if not women? Who else could assure the rights of succession, since a child issued from a single womb like a plant sprouting from a unique plot of earth, be that plot inundated by countless rains and flooded by innumerable rivers. And while men went their own way, as free of roots as pollen, it was Motherhood, the central constancy of the family hearth, which insured a permanent port of haven in a world of confusion and upheaval.

Yet by manipulating Orestes, by allowing him to murder his mother, Zeus would alter definitively the order of things. Were Orestes not punished with death, the power of women on Earth--and subsequently in Heaven--would cease. For Hera the target was clear: it was the survival of matriarchy against the growing menace of *man*kind, and all the promiscuity, irresponsibility and savagery inherent in males, a sub-race those acts and motivations exuded from the blind, incoherent forces gathered at their loins.

Hera thought of the terrible concordance of events which had come together--like the staggeringly freakish alignment of the planets--to bring havoc on the sex of which she was the heavenly protectress. First there was Zeus, and his will of domination over Heaven, Earth and Ocean. He had already taken up with Ganymede and none of the Olympians was blind to the use he made of *him*. Then there was Apollo, who would relegate women to the role of unpaid child-breeders, while encouraging men to form homo-erotic bonds, on the bases of which they could play philosophical games between intellectual, physical and sexual equals. Already Apollo had pushed the earthly Alcmaeon to kill his mother, Eriphyle, who had accepted a bribe in exchange for betraying her city. This first matricide Hera had avenged by turning the Erinnys against Alcmaeon, monsters with dog heads, bat wings and serpent hair. The Erinnys had torn Alcmaeon limb from limb, leaving not enough for decent burial. This was also the fate Hera had in mind for Orestes who was shacked up with his lover Pylades. It was the only way she would be able to shield her privileges. Should Orestes not be destroyed by the Erinnys, should he survive, Hera herself would succumb, and with her all womankind would know a night as eternal as that threatening Greece from the lawless hordes of savages spread throughout the steppe lands beyond its borders. Finally, there was all that silly talk about Zeus giving birth, even if it was true that Dionysos had been cut from his thigh, and Athena freed from his head through the breach Hephaestus had rent with his chisel and hammer.

Hera did not succeed and from hereon male might and lust would rule the world. Eventually Orestes returned to Mycenae where he became king, alongside Pylades. When they died their bodies were carried to Sparta where a cult to them was initiated in the strangest of rites. Boys were bound to an altar and flogged until their blood splattered the marble surface in symbolism of earlier human sacrifices. Because the whippings were in honor of Apollo, the participating boys vied with each other to see which of them could accept the greater suffering without loss of face, and shed the most blood without loss of life. The frenzy of their zealotry, aided by the hallucinogens they drank to make the pain bearable, produced an erotic arousal of frenetic intensity and blood-gorged phalli that threatened to burst. The resulting ejaculations, mixed with the streams of blood, came to symbolize the fecundity of the people, and the fertility of their lands. (3)

Other consequences of Clytemnestra's murder were to follow. On Olympus itself the godhead was divided between the sexes, six chairs around the holy table for women, six for men. But the murder of Clytaemnestra opened the gates for those who sought the rule of men. Dionysus led the way by taking Hestia's seat at the hallowed table, an act Zeus let pass in silence. And Apollo, never missing an opportunity to promote male superiority and the primacy of male-to-male relations, decreed, by way of Euripides, that ''a woman was now no more than an inert furrow into which a man could expulse his seed.''

This, then, takes care of the children of Pelops: Atreus, Thyestes, Agamemnon, Aegisthus, Menelaus and Orestes. With the deaths of them all, the curses of Myrtilus and Thyestes came to an end.

THE WORLD'S FIRST BOY-LOVE EVANGELIST: ORPHEUS

Male-to-male friendships had its first evangelist, Orpheus. Like the first Christian disciples who didn't shun from going, literally, into the lion's mouth in Rome, Orpheus chose one of the most barbarous regions to have ever existed, Thrace, to introduce boy-love. This is his story.

Orpheus could charm the spots off a leopard. With his lyre and beautiful voice streams ceased to trickle, rocks cried and trees danced, wrote Simonides of Ceos. Birds interrupted their songs, claims Pindar. The Oracle of Delphi told Jason to include Orpheus among the Argonauts, which he was thankful for doing as no ship had ever been able to sail pass the Sirens, whose songs enticed sailors to shipwreck against their rocky home. But Orpheus played his lyre so wonderfully that the sounds from the Sirens never reached the men's ears, so enhanced were they by Orpheus' music.

On his wedding day his wife Eurydice was bitten by a snake and died. At her funeral Orpheus' mournful songs caused even the gods to weep. They suggested that he go to the slime-walled caverns of the Underworld and beg Hades for her return. So he went to the river Styx where he charmed Hades' watchdog, the three-headed Cerberus, to let him through to Chiron, the ferryman who paddled the newly deceased across the vile waters from which none returned. Frightened bats fought for hiding places as Orpheus made his way through the most inaccessible, putrid side-shafts, the hotbed of the death maggots, to Hades' throne. There, his playing and singing softened the rock-hard heart of the foulest of the gods, he who placed his foot on the chests of brave warriors and tore out their souls from their still-warm bodies. Hades permitted him to return to the Upperworld with his sweetheart, as long as he never looked back to make certain she was indeed following. At the entrance, though, he did turn his head, in time to see her vanish into the noisome mists.

Decided to never again undergo such pain, he transferred his love to boys--boys not men--boys whose early flowering and springtime, says Ovid, is so brief. He spent three years as Apollo's priest at Delphi where he readied himself to propagate the cult of the god of Light. Apollo told him about Hyacinth and the joy of running, swimming and laughing with carefree lads, exercising, imparting knowledge and rolling in the deep grass with sturdy, cornfed bucks as frisky and proud as stallions. As Orpheus was Apollo's best acolyte, Apollo sent him to the most difficult land in Greece, that of the Thracians, a barbarous people who went stark naked because they knew of the contamination that filthy clothing brought to wounds received in warfare. He revealed to them that the love of boys kept one eternally young, thanks to their innocence, and it is said that he showed the way by having many, many beloveds. He introduced the cult of Apollo, to the disgust of the vile Maenads, the fanatical followers of Dionysus. He made the Thracians exchange cannibalism for fruit, and human sacrifice for rites similar to that of the Spartans, rites far less savage than human flesh eating but far more erotic too. He helped them found towns and organize themselves. The Thracians made huge strides, even if they still remained more heathen than other Greeks. The proof is that even in more recent times, during the life of Alcibiades, Athens had engaged Thracians as mercenaries but were forced to let them return home without pay because the city had gone bankrupt. The Thracians returned through Boeotia, a land to the north of Athens. Along the way they massacred every living thing, Thucydides tells us, men, women and children, boys in their schools and beasts of burden. "Nothing was so unexpected and loathsome," ends Thucydides, whose disgust is easily felt and seconded. (2)

It was then that Orpheus undertook the voyage as an Argonaut, during which he met the young and handsome Calais, "a boy he loved," according to the poet Phanocles. But their idyll was not to last. This time it wasn't the youth who died but Orpheus himself. He returned to Thrace with Calais and found that the Thracians had backslid. Most had returned to the rites of the Maenads, Dionysian maidens who enticed the Thracians into wild orgies when under the influence of their god's wine. The Maenads immediately attempted to entice Orpheus and Calais with naked breasts and spread thighs, but met only disgust from the man and the boy. In revenge they fell on Orpheus with tooth and nail, tearing him to pieces. Fleet footed Calais escaped and joined his twin brother Zetes. They were later killed by Heracles who accused them both of hindering him when he went off in search of *his* beloved, Hylas. The Muses gathered up the remains of Orpheus and buried them at the foot of Mount Olympus where nightingales eternally sing over his grave. His lyre was placed in the heavens as a constellation. His soul was reunited with that of Calais in the Elysian Fields.

The lyre is often represented in the hands of handsome lads on Greek pottery, an indication that they were followers of Apollo and adepts of his male-to-male/boy sexuality.

HYLAS

Hylas was a looker and as the poet Theocritus (300 B.C.) tells us, "We mortals were not the first to see beauty in what is beautiful. Even the warrior Heracles who defeated the savage Nemean lion loved a boy, the handsome Hylas, he whose hair hung down in golden curls. He was like a father to the splendid lad, teaching him how to become a mighty man." But before we get to Hylas, here's the story about the Nemean lion: The

Nemean lion was no common lion. From Herodotus we learn that lions were existent in Greece up to 100 B.C. This particular animal had fangs like daggers, claws like the sharpest swords and impregnable golden fur. It captured maidens that it held hostage in its lair to attract young warriors that the lion would slice to ribbons and devour. Now, Heracles was no poof. While passing through Thebes he slept, during a single night, with the forty-nine virgin daughters of the same father. The fiftieth daughter refused him and in anger he sentenced her to remain a virgin until the end of her life, every girl's nightmare. With women he had orgasms, we're told, with boys and men he made love. So Heracles was just passing through Nemea when he came upon a splendid lad, a shepherd, Molorchos, who had lost his dad to the lion. He asked Heracles to give him a hand in killing it but when Heracles balked, the boy said that if he didn't do what he asked in thirty days, he would sacrifice himself on the altar of Zeus. The lad himself was no tyro to boy-love, and made it clear to the hero what his reward would be if, at the end of the same period, he returned alive and lusty, ready to play night games. Like Apollo, Heracles preferred happy-go-lucky kids because they never asked for anything in return for a few minutes under Heracles' iron-strong body, a far cry from women you always had to pay, like the theater, to enter. Heracles managed to club the animal to death and then, admiring its pelt, decided it would be perfect to clothe him. But the fur couldn't be cut with any instrument Heracles used against it. Molorchos, now by his side, suggested that Heracles use the lion's own claws to skin the animal, which was exactly what Heracles did. He threw the pelt over his shoulder and was never without it from then on.

That's what he was wearing when he joined the Argonauts and came upon Hylas who was a crewmember. As Theocritus wrote, ''Brave Hylas, in the flower of youth, went aboard the Argos, to carry Jason's arrows and guard his bow.'' Soon he would be Heracles' squire, carrying Heracles' bow and arrows. It was their second meeting and all the men agreed that they formed the perfect couple, Heracles muscle bound and deeply tanned, Hylas slim waisted and light skinned. During their first meeting, when Hylas was just a kid, Heracles killed his father when he objected to Heracles slaughtering one of his bulls. This was a pitiful reason for murder, but Heracles was never known for his subtlety. For example, even in his youth he went whole hog: Laomedon, king of Troy, had upset Poseidon who sent a snakelike monster to destroy the Trojans. Laomedon sent an embassy to the Oracle at Delphi to find out how the Trojans could protect their citizens. The Oracle instructed the king to sacrifice his daughter Hesione. In this way, promised the Oracle, Poseidon would be appeased.

Laomedon complied. Hesione was tied to a boulder overlooking the sea while the Trojans retreated into the safety of the walls. Among them, however, was a foreigner, Heracles, who offered to save Laomedon's daughter and destroy the sea monster if Laomedon would give him Hesione in marriage. The king agreed.

With sword in hand, Heracles was waiting when the beast slithered out of the Hellespont's gray, eddy-wracked waters onto the sandy beach where Hesione was bound like Prometheus. Heracles slew the tentacled creature and cut Hesione free. She was taken in hand by her chirping maidens while Heracles, his chest bloated with self-importance, sought a meeting with the king. But instead, the palace guard led him out of the country and told him that if he returned it would be under pain of death.

Heracles did return, however, this time with his friend Telamon, king of Salamis, and a great army. Catching the Trojans unaware, they rushed through Troy's open gates and sacked the city, killing Laomedon and all his sons except the youngest, Prince Priam. Priam as only eight when he met Heracles coming from his father's throne room, Laomedon's decapitated head held by the hair in one hand, his blood still wet on Heracles' sword held in the other. Understanding the fate awaiting him, the child tried to placate Heracles' anger by offering to make him king of Troy.

The lusty Heracles broke into laughter. He awarded the crown to the child for his levelheadedness, and gave Hesione to Telamon for his wife. He stripped Troy of all gold and silver, took enough Trojan women to satisfy his soldiers and returned to Greece. (1)

So when Heracles met up with the boy whose father he'd killed, he expected the worst, but got the best. Hylas had been abused by his father when young, and was glad to learn how to become a warrior at Heracles' side. They spent enough time together for both to be extremely appreciative of the other, so when Hylas, off to get some water for the ship's crew, suddenly vanished, Heracles, mad with fear that he had been waylaid by robbers, went off looking for him. He ordered the *Argo* to wait for his return but when two captains, Calais and Zetes, refused, he killed them both. It turned out that Hylas had wandered to a spring guarded by nymphs, one of whom, Mysia, fell in love with the boy. As he reached over to fill his amphor she reached up for a kiss. Hylas lost his balance and Mysia, thinking he dived in thanks to his willingness to offer her more, pulled him down to her watery abode, unaware that by doing so she would kill him.

The end of Heracles was markedly unworthy of a hero of the Twelve Labors and an Argonaut. One day he was wandering around the countryside with his wife when he came upon a rampant river. A seemingly gentle Centaur named Nessus offered to carry Heracles' wife, Deianeira, across it. Heracles thanked him and began to swim to the other side, confident that Nessus was following with Deianeira on his back. When Heracles reached the opposite bank, however, he was aghast to see his wife still on the further shore, in the clutches of the Centaur who had straddled her.

Heracles shot an arrow across the river that pierced Nessus in the neck, causing him to withdraw at the moment of his pleasure, and ejaculate over Deianeira's thighs. Before dying, the Centaur, who knew of Heracles' fondness for both sexes, told Deianeira that if she dipped Heracles' shirt in a mixture made from the Centaur's blood and seed, she would never have to worry about her husband being unfaithful again. Deianeira took the advice, putting the liquids in a jar and hiding it.

Years later, Deianeira, now old, learned that Heracles was making a sacrifice at Zeus' temple in the company of still another young boy. Eaten by jealousy, she decided to use the Centaur's mixture as a love-potion to win him back. Heracles sent to Deianeira for a clean shirt to wear to the sacrifice. Deianeira took a new one from the chest and, with the aid of a piece of cloth, covered the shirt with the mixture. She then tossed the piece of cloth outside, and sent the shirt to her husband.

Moments later her attention was drawn to the sunlit courtyard by something blazing like reflecting bronze. There she saw the piece of cloth enveloped in fire. Realizing that the Centaur had tricked her, she sent to stop the shirt from being delivered to Heracles.

She was too late. Heracles was before Zeus' altar in his new shirt when the heat from the burning sacrifice caused it to erupt into flames. Seized by overpowering pain, he tried to pull away the garment. Only his own flesh, bleeding and corroding, came loose. Mad with suffering, he tore at himself until the bones of his bloody arms and pearl-white ribs were laid bare. To escape the agony, he begged his friends to place his body on a pyre so he could end his days before being turned into a mindless half-wit by the eroding fluid.

The pyre was built and Heracles placed on top, but no one dared to light it for fear lest he change his mind and strike him dead. By chance an unknown shepherd passing through consented to put a torch to the funeral pyre. This was Philoctetes, and in thanks Heracles gave him his bow and arrows. The swirling flames brought an end to the great hero and to his wife, Deianeira, who threw herself into the blaze out of grief.

CHAPTER FOUR

ACHILLES-PATROCLUS-TROILUS

Despite Achilles' immense superiority as a warrior over Patroclus, it was nonetheless Patroclus, as the older man, who had access to the most intimate parts of his beloved, Achilles. We'll begin this chapter with Patroclus at the court of King Lycomedes where Achilles' mother, Thetis, hid him from Odysseus and Agamemnon who had been told that they could not vanquish Troy without the boy:

Patroclus sat on a low marble bench beside a large square pool situated in the inner court of Lycomedes' palace. He had been bathing and was now allowing the warm late-afternoon sun to dry the rivulets of water running from his wet hair. He was gazing at the blue mosaic dolphin with its young rider on the bottom of the basin. Slowly he became aware of Phoenix' presence who had entered quietly and sorrowfully. As was proper, he put his hands in his lap to cover his nakedness. He turned to the old man who seemed troubled.

"Achilles is going to Troy," said Phoenix with great sadness. "He sent a servant to inform me that he is sailing tomorrow and wished me to accompany him"

"I thought he had decided not to go," said Patroclus, surprised.

"He obviously found an argument that decided him otherwise."

"How strange. I've never known him to go back on a decision once taken. Where did he go after talking with you?"

"He went to see his mother. She was with King Lycomedes. He must have hesitated before announcing himself, and in so doing overheard his mother and the king discussing him."

"What could they have been talking about to have caused such a sudden change of heart?" asked Patroclus.

"His destiny, although I'm not certain it was their conversation that persuaded him to shift ground."

For Patroclus, as for Achilles, Destiny was a sweet word, evoking images of fame and glory. But Phoenix knew the truth. Night had three children: black Chaos, remorseless Death, and hideous Destiny.

"Did you know, Phoenix, that I was at Helen's wedding, and one of her suitors? I will be obliged to join the Greek fleet immediately. I must tell Achilles."

"He already knows. The purpose of Odysseus' visit has become common knowledge throughout the entire city. He knows your honor obliges you to go to Troy, and he will follow."

"You say that as if you think he's changed his mind for my sake."

"Perhaps, but do not mention it. It is not a thing to talk about, even among yourselves. Just carry this proof of his affection with unspoken pride."

"And so I shall, Phoenix. But now I wish to find him."

"Then go, Patroclus, nothing keeps you here."

Achilles would go with Patroclus to Troy despite the folly of the expedition, the tutor lamented. He would fulfill the destiny that he now knew lay before him. That destiny, Phoenix understood, would be a beautiful death, a death that would spare him the demeaning ravages of age, and guarantee him forever the esteem of others in whose songs of praise he would find eternal life. It was the confirmation of that destiny, Phoenix surmised, that Achilles had overhead from behind the door concealing his weeping mother and the aged king.

Patroclus found Achilles in his room. Achilles was seated on a stool, unlacing his sandals. Patroclus knelt before him, took his foot, placed it on his thigh, and continued the unlacing.

"I will sail tomorrow with Odysseus," began Achilles. "I have been promised an important command." He hesitated. "We will share it together, if you agree?"

"Many will die at Troy. The Trojan priest Calchas has said that the Fates will be busy spinning, measuring and cutting."

"The Fates are beyond tampering with," asserted Achilles. "A man's time is his own."

"That is my consolation. Their decisions are beyond the meddlesome hands of men and gods. It is said that you will know great glory at Troy, but that you will pay the highest price."

"The highest price that I could pay for my glory would be to lose you," said Achilles, a tightness gripping his throat. "Do not make me think of such a finality. But it is one thing to fear death for those we love, another to fear it for itself. There is the story of the two young Argives renown for their prowess in athletics. Their mother wished to go to the festival of Hera but her oxen had wandered off and could not be found. The two boys, in a show of obeisance and piety, yoked themselves to her oxcart and pulled her ten full miles to the temple. Upon arrival they were immensely congratulated for so filial an act, and their mother highly praised for two such worthy sons. To demonstrate her gratitude, the mother sacrificed to Hera, asking the goddess to bestow her highest blessing on the boys. And so it was that after the feasting, they went into the temple and fell asleep, never to awaken again. Thereby do we know that death is more enviable than life."

"The goddess certainly had her reasons, but is it not a truth that we should search out neither death nor life, but accomplish both nobly?" asked Patroclus.

"Yes. But all the same one does hate Death for taking beyond our reach those we love. For that there is no consolation. Were I to lose you, I'm afraid the madness would descend upon me; I am fearful that I would dishonor your memory by my grief."

"Death and Sleep are brothers," said Patroclus, always armed with a story to educate his beloved. "There is nothing terrifying about Death. His role is not to kill, but to accompany the dead to the land of Hades. Yet these brothers are not twins. Sleep is gentle to mortals, invigorating those who allow his soothing hand to bring them momentary oblivion. Hard-hearted Death has a soul of iron. Those who fall into his grip never return from his dwelling. Ensnared in his black cloak, their kingdom becomes the land of eternal gloom."

Both arranged their clothes. Achilles slipped into the bed the first, and then Patroclus. He found his place against Achilles' side, his leg gently draped over his beloved's thighs. Did Patroclus foresee his coming fate, a fate he knew he held in common with others, as he held in common the happiness that filled his heart at this moment, a happiness that was his, but one that others had known before and would know again, and that long after he had become dust? He put his arm under his beloved's head and leaned over him. Silently he searched the blue eyes, and finding his answer, he kissed the parted lips. Then he moved his head back and with one breath blew out the oil lamp, bringing down night, a celestial curtain.

As Achilles became a man, he desired to find a boy to educate and train in warfare as Patroclus had educated and trained him, even though, later, Achilles' natural gifts made him superior to Patroclus in battle. Achilles had his eye on Troilus, but he had competition, as we see in this scene. Helen had been abducted by Paris and was now in Troy:

Helen emerged from the anteroom with Troilus, King Priam's son, a boy of thirteen, his arm in a sling. She wore a white pleated gown that fell to her sandaled feet. Unlike other women, her skin was bronzed, nearly as bronzed as Paris'. She was tall, her hair fell to her shoulders, and her eyes were as strikingly blue as her father Zeus'.

"I see you've met my little brother, Troilus," said Paris

She knelt before the boy and adjusted the cloth over his broken arm. "I saw him in the corridor. He reminded me of a little bird that I found in Sparta with a crippled wing. I took care of it for weeks until its wing healed and it flew away. How I envied it." She finished with the bandages. "There," she said, "run off little bird. I won't try to stop you, but I may envy you your freedom," she called after Troilus. "And don't forget what I told you!"

"What did you tell him?" asked Paris, taking a firm hold of her arm.

"He told me that when he became a man he would lay the world at my feet."

Paris scoffed.

"I told him that strong and handsome as he was, what had he better to do."

"Advice fit for grown men," floundered Paris.

Helen smiled, freed herself from his grasp, and strolled out of the throne room, leaving the others to stare at the eerie, gaping hole through which she vanished.

Helen was interested in more than the boy's arm. On his way to Troy Agamemnon killed one of Troy's supporters, King Tenes, on the island of Tenedos, visible from the heights of the city:

At that moment came a cry of alarm from outside the palace, and Priam rushed in from the hallway.

"It's Tenedos, Sons. The ship we sent has just returned. The Greeks have killed King Tenes and set fire to the city."

Both Hector and Paris bounded past Cassandra and wretched open the latticed door to the balcony. Paris was the first to see the couple in the shadows. Hector was the second. His stomach sickened at the outrage. Priam pushed past his sons, oblivious to the twosome lost to the obscurity. The old king took Hector's repulsion and Paris' distress as the anguish he himself felt over the fatality of the events on Tenedos. For across the Hellespont the island burned like a flaming volcano. All of Troy was enveloped in its bloodstained light. Still unseen by Priam, Helen had risen from her knees. Troilus, his boy prong sticking straight out, stooped to raise his chiton.

Knowing that the Delphic Oracle had decreed that Achilles was necessary if the Greeks hoped to destroy Troy, Troilus, now sixteen, the age the Greeks felt to be the most propitious for man-to-boy love, hid in Apollo's temple outside the walls of Troy, a site declared neutral territory for both warring factions. In hopes of discovering the secret to Achilles' invincibility, Troilus confronted him:

Helios sought in vain to disperse the black clouds that encumbered and subdued the snow-gray plain of Troy in their bleak shadows and numbing cold. The citadel rose ominously above the wind-swept Scamander, trickling soundlessly under a somber mantle of ice to the open sea. On the beach the men took shelter in tents and skin huts around small pit-fires. They wore rags and wrapped themselves with wool cloaks and sheep pelts. Few had ventured beyond the camp that winter, none had washed. The accumulation of filth in which they lived lay dormant, awaiting the suns' warmth to putrefy and spread death.

On a path leading from the shore inland strode Achilles, briskly making his way to a small hillock outside the walls of Troy, the temple of Apollo. There, inside the temple, stood Troilus, erect, his arms outstretched before the statue of Phrygian Apollo, god of Harmony, oracular Patron of Boys.

"Apollo, son of Zeus, ruler of Heaven and Earth, it is I, Troilus, son of Priam, king of Troy, who stand before you. Do you know me? At birth I was carried by my father in his own arms, naked and wailing, through the streets of Troy, that the people might see the last son of their king. Trojan men and women left their homes and shut their shops to behold their new prince. A procession was formed that followed my father through Troy's mighty gates to your hallowed temple in the shadow of the city's impregnable walls. The farmers left their plows and the fisherman their nets. Rivers of rejoicing men and women flowed to your temple, great Apollo. There, my father placed me on the altar still crimson from the morning's sacrifice. Calchas came forward with the sacred oil and dedicated me to your cult, thereby placing me under your vigilance and protection. Your code of honor became my own, divine Apollo, and I was conferred the yoke that symbolized subservience to your will.

"As a boy I was again brought before you, this time with the sweating sickness. Already my soul wandered the banks of the river Styx, and it was with despair that my father placed me once more upon your altar. Sacrifices were burned to you, god of Harmony; hymns were sung in your honor, 0 god of the Golden Mean; and in a blaze of glory you came before me. Enshrouded in fire you took me in our eternal arms and restored my strength; your lips were placed on mine, and my will to live was renewed. Your breath rekindled my own and I was revived. With your help, and leaning for unique support on the priest Calchas, I walked from the temple.

"How your praises were sung then, precious Apollo. How the people wept in thanks for your goodness! Fifty rams and fifty ewes were sacrificed; your altar was ablaze night and day for weeks.

"Do you remember dear Apollo, master and guide?

"Do you remember last spring when I entered your temple, a boy, on the threshold of manhood? I stood before you then as I am now, and with my own sword I offered you my first hair-cutting, a sign of obedience to your laws and a symbol of initiation into the rites of your order. You blessed my sword and shield, mighty Apollo, and from your temple I strode fully armed--a warning to our enemies that I had now become a man and a warrior.

"Do you know me now, just Apollo? It is I, Troilus, your creation and your servant.

"I come from tortuous dreams that obscure my vision; I come with secrets for your ears alone. Only you, greatest of Oracles, can lift the veil from before my eyes and permit me to see things that are and will be. In return, accept this sacrifice. It is a goat from my own herd; chosen by my own hands. It is I who cut its throat and placed it here. Take it, Apollo, and give me sight that I might understand the restless images that trouble my sleep.

"Last night the beautiful Helen came to me in a dream as she has every night since my brother Paris brought her from Sparta, eight years ago. She wore the same flowing gown, open at the bodice. Her naked breasts took on the color of bronze from the light of the candle in the wall-niche above my head. She went to the bedside chair where I had hastily thrown my tunic. Carefully folding it, she placed it neatly over the backrest. She smiled as she had every night, and sat on the edge of the bed beside me. My hands sought to caress the painted nipples, the access to which was her offering for my thirteenth birthday. I waited with abated breath her lips in the hollow of the blankets bunched at my waist, the warmth of which would still my fervor and bring renewed sleep. But this time Helen's mouth did not bring me blissful relief, this time her lips parted and she spoke. Helen had never spoken before, except in reality, and then only to laugh at my timidity and make fun of my callowness. She was always saying that a boy my size was capable of the acts of men. I was thusly surprised when words came from her mouth, but my surprise turned to astonishment when I realized the voice was not that of Helen. For many moments I lay baffled until, piercing the obscurity of my room I saw that she had left a young man at my door to stand guard. I remember thinking how silly it was keeping watch over a door in the safety of a dream. Yet it was thanks to the youth and his quiver of arrows that I recognized my visitor as Aphrodite, and her protector as Eros.

" 'There is a new and dreadful danger within Troy,' she said. 'Hera has hardened Hector's resolve to end the war. She has convinced him that Troy can still be saved if Helen is returned to Menelaus. She has told him that the Greeks are tired of fighting and will sail home without demanding reparations--Helen alone will be the price of their going. Hera has organized a meeting in Apollo's temple between Achilles and Hector to conclude a treaty. Hector's reward will be peace for his country, his people, his wife and his son. Achilles' reward will be marriage to Polyxena, your half-sister, in this life, and the possession of the fair Helen in the hereafter.

" 'Now I, Aphrodite, order Troilus to prevent the betrayal of Troy by subverting any accord reached between Hector and Achilles, thus making you guardian of Helen. In exchange, I give you my solemn promise that Troy will vanquish her enemies and live in honor for untold millenniums in the hearts and imaginations of future civilizations. Further, I renew my pledge that Helen will retain her nuptial bond with Prince Paris, her rightful husband, but that she will yield to implacable Passion by becoming the mistress of her savior, Prince Troilus.'

"In this way did she speak, dear Apollo, and I would be there with her still had Eos not risen blushing in the East, filling my room with her coral light and erasing Night who had given form to my visitors.

"I therefore ask your help, just Apollo. I ask you to give me the strength to be Troy's protector and Helen's suitor. Let me defeat through cunning or force the noble Achilles so that I and all Trojans will once again know freedom as we did before the coming of the Greeks. But if it be my destiny to fail, dearest Apollo, and Troy be destroyed, then I beg of you:

strike down every last Greek as retribution for depriving unborn generations of Trojans the joy of gazing over the beauty of the world from Troy's great walls, and the marvel of finding first love as was known by me, Troilus, for Helen."

"You've grown."

Troilus spun around to find Achilles at the temple door. "The great Achilles knows me?"

"I have seen you often in battle."

"I was on the field for the first time only last summer."

"You did not go unnoticed."

Troilus surveyed his enemy, this the greatest of the Greek warriors. He wished to face him as a man, yet in his heart he felt the turmoil of a cornered boar, waiting for a chance to charge and gore, or break and run. "Have you come as a friend?"

"Yes." Achilles sensed the dilemma and sought to skirt it.

"Do your plans include Helen?"

"Troy is being destroyed, Troilus, as is Greece. The pretext for that destruction is Helen. Our survival depends on her removal."

"If she's that dangerous, why do you risk having her returned to her husband? Aren't you afraid Chaos will follow her back to Greece to wreak havoc there?"

"Helen is no more than the instrument of the gods, Troilus. She's dangerous because Destiny has conspired in a number of uncanny ways to place her in the center of a conflict which began long before the present war. First, the gods were angered for some obscure reason involving Paris, Hera, Aphrodite and Athena; next, the Greeks settled upon war ostensibly to retrieve Helen, but covertly for Troy' riches and strategic position on the Hellespont; and lastly, even the very hill upon which Troy was built is contriving to throw the city off, in accordance to a curse laid down in times forgotten. If this war should continue, Troilus, Troy will fall and Greece will be so depleted of her young leaders that she may enter an age of regression so black and stagnant as to never reemerge. To return Helen is to abort the paltry intrigues of gods and men, thereby heralding an age of Justice--and not even Helen, Troilus, is as beautiful as Justice."

"Where was Justice when Helen was allotted to Menelaus against her own will? In the name of what justice have Trojan cities been pillaged and their populations massacred? And who took part in those massacres, if not Achilles-of-the-blue-eyes?"

"Let's not overlook the facts," said Achilles, showing anger. "Helen was abducted by a Trojan prince. If there is fault, it lies with Troy."

"My Aunt Hesione was carried off by the Greek Heracles and given to his friend Telamon like one casts away a worn pair of sandals..."

"Why open old wound...?"

"...and Troy was burned to the ground. What was Justice doing then?" asked Troilus, his face flushed by the memory of the wrongs that pass from generation to generation like worthless heirlooms. "It is known by all that Justice stands to the left of Zeus and is at his beck and call: Zeus' every word is an order for her to obey. There is no weighing of right and mercy on her scales; only self-interest and whim are the notes played on her lyre."

"If you cannot see Justice in all men, admit, at least, that she can be found in some of us personally, like honor."

"That's why I'm going to protect Helen. Paris can't be counted on to do it and Hector's always wanted to send her back. What chance does Helen have to make up her own mind? She was forced to come here and she'll be forced to leave. But I'll stand up for her. Father won't dare send her back if he feels that my life hangs in the balance. My fate is Troy's fate. If I'm allowed to die, and Helen is turned over to the Greeks, then the city will deserve its destruction."

"Helen has taught you to love, but you are sad. The greatest happiness is to win the love of another. You will never win Helen's.

"What counts is the love we can offer, not the love we receive."

"Were you to come to Greece you would forget Helen. There, I would awaken your heart to the art of combat, and as one of my companions you would learn that friendship is of far greater value than momentary passion."

"Are all Greeks as hospitable as Achilles? Why should I put my trust in you and leave my homeland?"

"I've come as a friend, Troilus, to end this war. Like valiant Heracles of old who sailed these shores to free the fair Hesione from the sea monster's grip, so have I come to rescue you. But this is not the first time, prince, that I have tried to save you from Death's embrace. Years ago, at the time of your sickness, you were carried to this very temple. It was I who begged the god to spare you. Apollo heard my prayer, and incredibly you stood and walked through these doors, for I had promised the god my life for yours. Today I again wish to preserve that life."

"I am a Trojan, Achilles, and will remain with my people and fight for my own survival as well as theirs. I do not need nor want your friendship. Remember in further meetings that I am a warrior and Helen's suitor. Beyond those two requisites there is nothing left for us to discuss." He passed behind Achilles who remained facing Apollo, trusting his back to the boy. Troilus couldn't help marveling at shoulders twice the breadth of his own. The sword arm seemed knotted in overlapping muscles, the left appeared atrophied in comparison. "I'm now returning to Troy to do everything in my power to thwart your plans."

His last words were pronounced as he disappeared from view. Achilles turned to watch him run off and then again faced the statue of Apollo.

"Please, god, give me the wisdom to convince him that I am his people's only hope. Make him understand, dear lord, that the cost of a Greek victory would be his priceless blood at the end of a Greek sword."

But the boy later returned to the temple where he hid behind the statue of Apollo. He had sent his sister Polyxena in hopes that she would be able to discover where, on Achilles' body, he was vulnerable. She did so. Achilles revealed the secret, that Polyxena later confided to Paris:

Polyxena left the temple and Achilles turned to the statue of Apollo.

"The time has come, dear god; each of us is approaching the fulfillment of his Destiny: Troilus and his hopeless love; Hector, whose only wish is to be a father to his son; and Polyxena, so concerned for the safety of her brother and peace for her city. As for me, I know that the completion of my task is near, I ask only that it be nobly done. And the others? What is the fate of Priam and Hecabe, Andromache and Cassandra? And on the Greek side, that of Agamemnon, Nestor, Odysseus and Calchas? How many of them will return to their homes?"

Achilles looked out through the open temple doors upon the fortress city. A thought struck him: "Why must there be war? Soon we will all be dead, and nothing will be left of Troy but the aimless wandering of homeless ghosts, fighting as phantoms long-ago battles, no longer but whispers through wind-warped grass. If my mother had succeeded in making me a god and one day someone were to ask me to name the most courageous of creatures, I would answer Man, for he lives in the knowledge that he must grow old and die. Yet while the waning sun still warms our souls, the innocent must be protected."

Achilles thought in silence a few moments, and then addressed Troilus.

"It's time that we talked, Son."

Troilus stood up, his face flaming. Achilles was pained for the boy, but was aware of the little guidance he had received from his elders in time of mortal conflict.

"Will you give up Helen and come back to Greece with me?" asked Achilles, suspended over an abyss.

"It's rather the abduction of Helen in reverse, is it not?" smirked the boy, who had a Trojan's amused condescension for Achilles' form of frailty, a frailty that made him more vulnerable than the secret to his immortality.

Achilles could not let his humiliation go on. Nothing more was left to him where but a moment before everything had still been possible. In a matter of seconds his life had swung full circle and the extremes of his existence had come together and locked; the cycle was complete; Achilles was free.

"Then what do you want, Troilus?" he asked, quietly.

"You know the answer to that."

"She's in the palace. Go to her."

"Not for a night; for always."

"And Troy?"

"The Destiny of a city is that of her inhabitants."

"Things have gone too far for you to be able to alter them. Offer your love to another."

"I love Helen and she loves me. She's proved that dozens of times in the privacy of my rooms."

"She is surely touched by your beauty."

"What is love, if not the longing for the beautiful?"

"Sooner or later she will be returned to Menelaus."

"What should I do then?" smirked Troilus, expecting Achilles to invite him again to Greece.

"Spend your life in search of the beauty of which you speak."

"For how long?"

"So long as you do not regard death as better than life."

"And Helen?"

"Let her be sent to Sparta."

"If she's as redoubtable as you make her out to be, why do you risk sending her back?"

"Sparta is Greece's backwoods. Once in the mountain highlands she'll be cut off from the world. In Sparta Helen will be one beautiful woman among many others that Destiny could have chosen to entice Paris. Spartans don't put up with nonsense. At home Helen's fame will dissipate in the daily washing, scrubbing, cooking and childbearing that is as much demanded of a queen as of the most common citizen. She too will know indifference and neglect. She too will know age and oblivion."

"Helen deserves a better Fate."

"I don't think one can blame Fate for neglecting Helen, Troilus. She had the luck of being born a princess and marrying the wealthy Menelaus. In Sparta she ruled as queen, her power extending over the palace as well as the battalion of Spartans who sought the king's influence by taking the short cut through his wife's thighs."

Troilus drew his sword. "I'll make you regret that," he stammered. "I won't let you leave the temple. I'll block your way."

"You are strong, Troilus, but I am stronger. I will make you obey me without having to harm you. Only the weak are dangerous: their lack of moral strength makes them turn to deceit and treachery."

"You underestimate me, Achilles..."

"I respect your resolve, Troilus, and I know that you mean what you say. But I repeat, I'm determined to keep you from harming yourself."

"I call upon Apollo to be my witness," stormed Troilus. "I will fight for Helen to the death."

Alas, Apollo stood mute. He too loved Troilus, but only upon the freshly turned earth over the boy's corpse could the battle continue, and the hated Greeks be destroyed. Apollo mourned for Troilus, this innocent, this messenger of doom despite himself.

"All roads lead to death, Troilus. All. Make sure the one you're traveling is worth the taking. You won't have a chance to turn around and begin again."

"Is it your godly blood that gives you the right to ramble?"

"In your thrashings to keep Helen you resemble a drowning swimmer, Troilus. I repeat. I won't let you go under."

"Menelaus loves Helen and he doesn't seem to be drowning."

"Menelaus is nothing but a jilted husband, and in time he will only be known as such--if he's remembered even for that. There's no distinction in being cuckolded when one's wife is Helen."

Troilus flushed. "You said you were going to protect me from myself. Well go ahead, show me!" he cried out as he lunged towards Achilles. Achilles' mouth dropped in surprise, and only his war-tuned reflexes saved him from being pierced. He sprang aside and drew his own sword.

"You're being a fool, Troilus. You're not going to be able to get at me again with your sword and I'm not going to spill your blood with mine. To continue is senseless."

"But what a lesson for me!" shouted Troilus, his face red with fury. "Who wouldn't pay dearly to go a round with the great Achilles. What an occasion to pick up some pointers," he said, as he lunged again. His sword was easily struck to one side by Achilles'.

"You can be glad to get a free lesson," said the Greek. "You're the only man who will ever walk away alive to tell the tale."

"Save your gifts and your breath, the moment of my glory is enough," he exulted as he plunged toward Achilles. But this time Troilus threw aside his weapon, drawing Achilles' attention as it skittered across the marble tiles, and hurled his body forward, impaling himself on the Greek's outstretched sword. For an instant they stood facing each other. Then the boy, clutching Achilles, slowly slipped to the ground. Achilles accompanied the movement until he was on his knees, Troilus' head against his chest. He brushed the matted locks from the boy's forehead. Passing his hand over the still-flushed cheeks, he smoothed away the sweat that formed on the slopes of the boy's nose.

"I'll come back to haunt you," whispered Troilus. A trickle of blood formed at his mouth and ran down his chin and throat. Achilles tried to staunch it with the sleeve of his tunic, but like a stream whose destiny was the sea, it would not be checked. Troilus closed his eyes and seemed to have fallen asleep. Then with a sudden thrust his body was shaken by spasms; every muscle was contracted as if the lad were trying to right himself.

Achilles held to him with all his force to keep them both from falling over. Troilus opened his eyes on the statue of weeping Apollo, moved his lips as in prayer or adieu, and was dead.

Achilles cried softly for many moments before laying the boy's head on the cold stones and fleeing back to the ships.

It was Hector and Helen who found the boy, and all Troy mourned the young god snatched from life like a soaring eagle felled on its flight to the sun.

After a disagreement with Agamemnon Achilles refused to enter combat. His lover Patroclus convinces his beloved to let him wear his armor in the belief that when the Trojans see it, they will give up the fight:

Down at the far end of the beach Achilles and Patroclus came to an agreement.

"You can take my armor and the chariot and lead the Myrmidons into combat," said Achilles, "but you've promised to do no more than drive the Trojans away from the boats."

"When they see me dressed as you, they'll clear out quickly enough," answered Patroclus. "No one's so crazy as to come up against the mighty Achilles--they'll scatter like a bunch of eunuchs."

"Under no condition are you to go farther than the ships," insisted Achilles gravely. "When you see that the Trojan's have turned back, you return."

Achilles helped his friend don his golden breastplate and greaves with their silver buckles, the everlasting workmanship of Immortal Hephaestus. He fitted the gold shield to Patroclus' arm and strapped the silver-handled bronze sword over his left shoulder. Then, for an uneasy moment, they stood in silence facing each other. At last Achilles made a movement forward. Patroclus bit his lower lip, stopping his friend by grasping his right wrist. Achilles saw the trickle of blood run from the corner of Patroclus' mouth and understood. He took his friend's wrist in his own hand and through the mystery of touch begged him to return unharmed. He then put his golden helmet into Patroclus' hands and led him to the camp of the Myrmidons. There, the troops--ready for combat after months of inaction--were entrusted to Patroclus' care. Achilles, wanting to take no chance with the lives of his troops and friend, repeated his orders that they were only to chase the Trojans away from the ships. The driver Automedon came up with Achilles' chariot and Patroclus stepped on behind him. Achilles handed up two spears and bade him farewell.

The moment the men pulled away, Achilles went into his hut and took a carved chalice from out the chest his mother had packed for him. He washed his hands and the chalice, filled it with his finest wine and went out into the courtyard to speak to Zeus. He slowly spilt his offering on the sand as he spoke.

"Dearest Father, I commit the precious life of my friend into your hands. He has taken my place in battle to bring help to our retreating troops, and to uphold my pledge not to fight as long as Agamemnon remains their commander. Patroclus is more to me, Father, than I am to myself. Without his presence, death would surely be a sweeter refuge than this world which brings only burdens as we approach the futility of old age. For the warmth of the sun, the blue horizon, the tepid waters that caress our homeland, the swaying fields of golden wheat that fill our stomachs at the end of a day's labor, the soft breeze that cools our brow, and the hills of grapes that soothe our dry lips, all these suffice when one is young and the earth is seen through the eyes of youth. But when one shares one's life with another, there is need of a deeper meaning, a greater understanding.

"You so decreed at the Beginning of Time that Man was not to live alone, Wise Father, and through your wisdom came the supreme happiness: life by the side of one's beloved. By living your word we are whole, Father, and in our minds and hearts you exist. For such is our hallowed pact: through your will we walk the bountiful Earth; and through our worship--and the prayers of our children and their children--you continue to endure, Father, forever and ever. You have offered us the gift of love, and we have granted you immortality. One day I will cease, Father, but you will go on. The fruit of my love will continue to call you Father, and worship your name. I will fulfill my duty, and you must fulfill yours. But let it not be now, the coming of the dark. Let me and my friend live on to know the depths of our love, and to continue to sing your praise.

"As a child, Father, Patroclus came to our house an orphan. Soon he was a friend and then a brother. Later, in the absence of Peleus, he became my companion and even my father. He has only me, and I him. Please dear god, Father of Justice, keep him from harm's touch. Show mercy to two of your children. I am not asking for eternity, Father, but just a final, fleeting moment of happiness."

Achilles poured out the last of the wine, and Olympian Zeus on high heard his prayer. Through the heavy folds of sleep the words reached his ears. He rose from the love-bed he shared with Ganymede, cast away the curtains of willow bows and pierced the bank of swirling clouds that hid Troy. Golden rays lit up the plain for the first time that day, and revealed Patroclus riding along the beach toward the place where the Trojans had breached the mound and set fire to the ships. Almighty Father wrapped the beloved friend of Achilles in a blaze of protective light and promised that it was not there that he would meet his end.

Patroclus had nearly reached the ships. He caused the Earth to shake and the mountains to explode in fire. The sun was blackened and the sea poured onto the beaches to douse the burning boats. Trojans and Greeks fell to their knees in awe and fear, each man with a fast prayer to Zeus-Savior on his lips. Only Patroclus was undaunted. Enveloped in light and with a bloodcurdling war cry resounding from his high-plumed helmet, he led the Myrmidons in attack. The Trojans mistook him for the mighty Achilles and scampered in full panic back over the Greeks' hastily flung-up walls. Father took pride in the noble Patroclus, and held his scales of Justice up for all the gods to witness his immutable decision to make Achilles' courageous friend the day's victor. How great, then, was his own deception when he saw the scales tipped slowly but immutably downward in opposition to Achilles' companion. It suddenly became clear to Zeus that above glorious life, with all awesome beauty and heartrending disappointment, hovered motherly Clotho, Aunt Lachesis and grandmotherly Atropos, spinning, measuring and snipping; and not even Zeus had sway over their eternal labor.

Father sat heavily on a nearby hill and put his great head in his weathered hands. "I cannot weep for Man," he thought. "To do so would be to continually flood the Earth. And how can I relieve Man's agony if everyone plots behind my back and bribes me with their love? Even the final decisions of life and death are beyond my power. All I can do, and do it I shall," he said, rising, "is make this day the most valiant in Patroclus' short life, and one that will bring him eternal renown for his bravery, while defending the honor of his friend."

So saying, Zeus snapped his orders to all concerned that Patroclus was to have his own way. And even the Fates, he hinted darkly, would be wise to slow up their work until the waning of the day.

On went the Trojans towards their own walls with Patroclus hot on their heels, slaying to the right and to the left. Pronoos was the first to be brought down and then Thestor, as Patroclus' spear broke through his jaw. Next came Erylaos whose head Patroclus split in two. Then fell Erymas, Amphoteros, Epaltes, Tlepolemos, Echos, Pyris, Ipheus, Euppos and Polymelos, valiant Trojans every one. Even Zeus' own son Sarpedon was killed by a javelin thrown through the heart. This grieved Almighty Father for he had greatly loved Laodemeia, Sarpedon's mother, and had carefully supervised his love-child's upbringing. Zeus dispatched Apollo to cleanse the blood-splattered body in the crystal waters of the Scamander. The boy was anointed with ambrosia and dressed in the finest garments before being handed over to Death. Zeus allowed himself a tear, since Sarpedon was half-immortal, and wished to curb Patroclus, his murderer, who meant less to him than his own blood. But bound by his word, he let the slaughter go on until Patroclus--forgetting Achilles' warning--came up to the citadel's mighty walls. So certain was his invincibility that even Hector took cover behind the Scaian Gates. Stragglers were cut down and left dying in the dust. Adrestos, Autonoos, Echeclos, Perimos, Megades, Epistor,

Melanippos, Elasos, Mulios and Pylartes all met death within reach of the lofty doors the Trojans had closed and barred in fear of Patroclus' dripping sword. When the last of those abandoned had been dispatched, the Greeks prepared to climb Troy's walls. Already siege ladders had been brought up and Patroclus led the Myrmidons to the top of the west ramparts.

And it was then and there that Zeus turned his back on the man he had brought within a hair's breadth of victory. He returned to Olympus to mourn Sarpedon, who had once told Zeus, "I would gladly have avoided the war if immortality and not old age and death were the prize offered the survivors. But since no one can escape Death, let honors come in glory, the glory that we can give to others, or the glory others can give to us." Father left the outcome in the hands of the only god still on the field, Apollo, the Trojans' friend.

Three times Patroclus climbed to the top of the ramparts, and three times Apollo pushed him back. And so they would have continued until the arrival of Night if the Fates hadn't signaled Apollo from afar that the end of Patroclus' allotted length of wool was nearing the snippers. The god shoved the ladder away one last time and went down to find Hector. Taking the form of one of the guards, Asios, Apollo addressed the prince: "There's no reason to he afraid, Hector. That's not Achilles out there, it's Patroclus."

"It may he Patroclus as you say, my friend, but only a fool would go up against him as invincible as he is now."

"You won't be alone," insisted Asios. "Apollo will be there to disarm him."

"How do you know that?" demanded Hector, turning towards the guard.

"It was Apollo who stopped Patroclus from getting a foothold on the ramparts. Put your faith in him, Prince Hector. He loves the Trojans and won't let them down."

Hector saw from the piercing eyes that the speaker was Apollo himself. He therefore set off immediately through the Scaian Gates to confront Patroclus.

Outside, the Myrmidons were joined by reinforcements. Agamemnon, Menelaus, and Odysseus came up with their troops, as did Nestor, Idomeneus, Diomedes and the other captains. To their surprise, they saw that the Trojans, who were fleeing from them just hours before, were now coming out to engage battle. Neither side had time to form up into correct formations before becoming involved in a deadly melee. Spears were impossible in such close quarters and even swords were used with difficulty. Daggers were more efficient, but the soldiers used them badly, through lack of practice, and most of the thrusts produced superficial injuries rather than mortal wounds. For that reason Apollo decided to cut Patroclus off from his troops.

Under the cloak of invisibility he came up and pulled Patroclus, a final time, from the walls. Patroclus hit the ground, shattering Achilles' spear and breaking the shield. He tried to regain his feet but Apollo gave him another slap that sent him sprawling back into the trodden dust. Achilles' breastplate rolled gently from Patroclus' side. Still again the young prince sought to rise, but in vain. Apollo gave him one last shove that drove him clear of his fighting comrades and knocked the golden helmet from his stunned head. The boy's matted hair lay in ripples over his brow, and sweat blurred his half-closed eyes. Numbly he pushed himself to his hands and knees, but the blows from the Immortal god had overwhelmed him.

Never again would he ride by Achilles' side, or listen for his friend's familiar steps coming up the beach, or hold him when fear swept his restive dreams. Already Death was ascending to claim the body, still warm and unmarked. Death regretted the work the Fates had dealt him, yet his role was not the worst: for it was not he, nor Man, nor the Immortals, nor Helios, nor any living thing that would see Patroclus lose his beauty and fall into dust: the final witness would be the still, solitary, anonymous grave.

Patroclus tried to rise; Death drew nearer; and Hector broke away from the entangled pack and approached the prince on running feet, his spear poised tightly against his side. Patroclus turned his chest and arched his body towards the blurred warmth of the midday sun which enclosed his head in a halo, his arms outstretched as if to welcome Achilles, not the quickly advancing Trojan. And it was then, on his knees, his body open to the sun and his friend, that Hector planted his spear in the taut muscles of the abdomen, at the place where he had first received precious life.

Menelaus saw Patroclus fall the moment that Atropos snipped his cord. He sent Antilochos to tell Achilles. Antilochos rode across the plain and after an hour arrived in front of Achilles' hut. He was crying, poor man, for he had loved his companion, and he was afraid for his own life lest Achilles in a wild frenzy of agony cut his throat for being the bearer of such news.

Achilles came from out his hut and stood glassy-eyed as Antilochos bore the evil tidings. Achilles stared unspeaking for seemingly endless moments and then collapsed to the beach like a marionette cut from its strings. A groan, wrenching and hollow, formed within the deepest recesses of his soul as he became aware of the full horror of his loss. And the wail that left his lips sounded the death keel for a thousand men and heralded the end of a nation, a friendship, a love and the will to live. Antilochos knelt before his stricken commander and grasped Achilles' hands tightly in his for fear that in his fury Achilles would do himself or Antilochos harm.

"Weep for Patroclus, Antilochos," cried Achilles, "not for your own life. It is not you who will feel the brunt of my sword!"

Automedon came in from battle on Achilles' chariot behind the two immortal steeds, Xanthos and Balios. Achilles jumped on to go after Patroclus' body. Naked but for a borrowed sword that hung from a strap over his right shoulder and two spears, one in hand and one strapped to the chariot, Achilles swept across the beach and headed inland with such haste that his chargers' hooves scarcely grazed the ground.

The gods would never forget the slaughter seen that day. At its end a thousand lads lay obscenely exposed to flies that dropped their maggots into festering sword gashes and vulture-torn muscle; all honor and decency-- even the modesty of the tomb-- were denied them.

Before the gates of Troy Menelaus and Aias succeeded in wresting the body of Patroclus away from Hector. Back to the shore they rode, past Trojans running blindly before the approach of Achilles. Achilles saw Menelaus' chariot racing by and guessed at its hapless passenger. He broke off the fighting and followed it to the Greek camp. Menelaus wished to spare him the sight of Patroclus' disfigured body, mercilessly fought over by Greeks and Trojans, the latter who wished to parade it naked and broken through the steep, winding streets of Troy. But Achilles forced his way to his friend, taking Patroclus in both arms and drawing him tightly to his chest. Sobbing, waving back and forth with his friend held against him like a nursing child, Achilles watched over him throughout the cold, bitter night.

Dawn found Achilles bent unmoving over Patroclus' corpse. In the raw, white light both bodies had so much the same waxen hue that his mother Thetis, coming up from her cave in Ocean, took them both for dead.

"Achilles?" she asked, tentatively.

"And so it is, Mother, that when the desire to live is most insatiable, we are called upon to die. My heart is broken from the loss of my friend; what a simple matter it now will be to wrench what remains of my soul from my breast.

"Do you and Father know that I love you? Will Cheiron the Centaur he able to unburden his heart after the loss of his adopted son? And Phoenix, who will be responsible for him now? And my son ... will he follow the path dictated by his heart, knowing that in the face of Death a life honorably lived is the only one worth the endeavor?"

"Achilles..." said Thetis, quietly, as if gently awaking a baby.

"To what end?" he asked. "In a century, we will all be gone; yes, even you, dear Mother, who stand beside me weeping--who shall be left to remember your sweet tears?

"The shadow of the tomb is upon me. Were it not for the revenge that is Patroclus' right, I would accompany him now to the Elysian Fields. But I must first meet with Hector and make him regret his crime. I hope he has lived well, for there will be no comfort for him beyond the grave."

Achilles rose to his feet. His mother kissed his neck and laid her head on his shoulder.

"I must release Patroclus to the maidens who will clean and wrap him in linen," he said. "We shall raise a pyre so his body will be spared defilement, and his soul will fly unhampered to the Kingdom of Hades and Persephone. Then will I meet Hector before Troy's invincible gates; then will our destinies unfold. No more will Achilles feel the comfort of a mother's embrace; no more will Hector know the love of a faithful wife. The cold earth will claim its due; into dust and oblivion our brief moment of existence--vital to us, so trivial to the gods--will ebb; and we will be no more. I am a coward Patroclus; would I have died before you, than live to avenge your loss." (1)

Homer tells us that Patroclus came to Achilles in a dream, ''I couldn't stand to have my bones buried apart from yours, but together, just as we grew up together. Let a single tomb hide the bones of us two in its embrace: the double-handed golden amphora that your dearest mother provided for you.'' (The moment Homer speaks it becomes clear why his genius has spanned the centuries.)

The camp began to stir. From Nestor's tent came Agamemnon, Calchas, Menelaus, Odysseus and the other captains, all of whom had held a wake for Patroclus throughout the long night. Each looked wan and unkempt. They bent with difficulty as they passed through the tent flaps, and straightened uncomfortably. They did not stand around, for they had worked out a plan throughout the weary hours. None dared to approach Achilles except Calchas, who had been delegated to the duty. He went to the young warrior and whispered quiet, tender words in his ear. The old priest's usual excitability had been drained by the numbing lack of sleep. He placed his hands on Achilles' arm, as much to support himself as to reassure the boy, and led him up the beach to the narrow path that led to Apollo's temple. Together they would spend the morning in prayer.

Nestor had Patroclus' corpse taken to the enclosure of waist-high stalks that surrounded the old king's tent. A group of servant maidens washed and oiled his skin, rinsed and combed his hair, dressed him in a white tunic and wrapped him in a wool sheet. The maidens had done what they could in the absence of his natural warmth, and the sweetness of his breath and the fragrance of his skin.

Odysseus was sent to the verdant lap of Mount Ida with a large detail to bring back logs for a funeral pyre. The trees were rapidly felled, branched and dragged back behind the soldiers' horses.

On a gently sloping plain behind the shore Aias and Teucer supervised the digging of a shallow pit in which the funeral pyre was to be raised and in which the offerings were to be burned. Agamemnon had given himself the job of getting together the sacrifice. He had requisitioned jars of honey, vine and oil; sheep, cattle and a covey of partridges; four horses, one of which had belonged to Patroclus; and two of Patroclus' hounds. Twelve Trojan captives were also to be slain. Agamemnon hoped that the amplitude of the endowment would persuade Achilles to renounce his decision to not commit himself and the Myrmidons to the siege of Troy.

Menelaus supervised the building of the pyre. The logs were placed in the shallow pit and crisscrossed to form a giant square the length and width of a ship. On the top, ten feet from the earth, a platform was built of planks.

From the heights of Olympus the Ruling Twelve descended on joyless clouds to the plain of Troy where they hung suspended in the darkened sky high above the site. The Winds, the Furies and the Planets joined them, as did Night, Day and Mother Earth; the Fates, the Cyclopes and the Dactyls; plus uncountable other lesser gods like the Stars, Moon and, alas!, Death.

Looking down on the plain that was wrapped in a warm blanket of autumn orange and gold, they saw the funeral procession drawing near the pyre.

The men marched slowly, each step in time to the haunting beat of the soldiers' swords striking against their shields. The Myrmidons led the procession. Six abreast and four hundred deep, they were dressed in full battle regalia. Patroclus was carried gently on the shoulders of Agamemnon, Odysseus, Diomedes, Idomeneus, Nestor, Calchas, Aias and Menelaus. Achilles led the Myrmidons. The rest of the troops took up the rear, forming a line a mile long.

From Troy's walls watched Priam, Hecabe, Antenor, Eiphobus, Helen and … Paris. Did it ever occur to the young fool that it was he the agent of such misery?

At the pyre, Achilles gave his eternal farewell to Patroclus. He did it simply, respecting even in death his lover's modesty. The corpse was lifted onto the platform. Below, into the gutters between the edge of the pit and the logs, the animals were sacrificed, the jars of food, oil and wine were emptied and the captured Trojans were condemned to die. Each of the twelve was on his knees facing the logs. Each had his hands roped behind his back. All waited their turn as Achilles himself passed behind, pushed his knee into their spines, pulled back their heads by the hair, and slit their throats with Patroclus' own dagger. Their lives, valiant manhood and beauty ebbed rapidly down their chests and formed puddles where they fell after being shoved into the pit. All the gods looked on sadly except Death, who was busy flittering from one victim to the next.

Then came the soldiers, each throwing in a gift or libation. Finally Achilles stood alone before the pyre with Antilochos to his right. He took Patroclus' dagger and cut off the sprig of his own hair. He climbed to the platform and laid it in Patroclus' folded hands. Antilochos stepped forward and handed Achilles a torch that he immediately threw into the straw between the logs. The Winds blew down from the clouds to help the fire get a sure start. Moments later it was a roaring blaze and in Hades, Patroclus, free at last, crossed over the Styx and onto the Elysian Fields. (1)

Achilles kills Hector and then confronts his own death:

And while a dirge went up behind the city's gates, Achilles kept his rendezvous with the Three Fates. He wandered through the brilliant morning--fresh and still--up to Apollo's temple on the nearby hill. Heroic Patroclus had found eternal rest; valiant Hector had passed Mankind's conclusive test; and now the final retribution was required: the death of the young god that Peleus had sired. For wise Achilles had embraced a life of worth; his every act had been nobly planned from birth. The end of the well-trodden path was now in sight; he had to step from hallowed Life into dreadful Night. Within the temple came Polyxena's command: the time to pay back Troilus was now at hand. Her brother Paris was supplied the secret key, to bold Achilles' godlike immortality.

Achilles was before the altar to be blessed; where Troilus had fallen, he too would find rest. For lurking in the shadows of the temple's room, were the foul, treacherous phantoms that meant his doom. He knelt before the statue that was cold and grim; Had all the gods forgotten and abandoned him? He asked Apollo if he knew his fearsome name; behind him Paris raised his bow and took firm aim. Achilles was aware of the uncanny still; his body trembled as he felt a piercing chill. Then came a sudden noise that shattered the vile dark; the lethal arrow went directly to its mark. Apollo guided it to stunned Achilles' heel: no one could change Apollo's hard, unbending will. Achilles, son of Thetis, was abruptly killed; and his Destiny everlastingly fulfilled.

Courageous Nestor found the body lost to Sleep; he bent his head uncaring of who would see him weep. The Myrmidons conveyed their king away on shields; aloft, they carried him across the autumn fields. No more would great Achilles feel the sun's presence; no more would brave Patroclus know love's sweet essence; no more would noble Hector watch his children bloom: the tomb would hold all three in its eternal gloom. The gods beheld Achilles be consumed by fire; in Troy, old Priam put the torch to Hector's pyre. Over the plain two funnels of smoke filled the air; both nations fell upon their knees in mournful prayer. The gods from Mount Olympus saw the rising flames; in the immortal stars they carved the heroes' names. Then Zeus, their souls, to Heaven did finally commend; and the Age of the Demigods came to an end. (1)

CHAPTER FIVE

THEMISTOCLES – ARISTEDES – STESILAUS

As Xerxes approached Athens two leaders of unsurpassed importance to the Athenians were preparing for battle. Battle against the king of the Persians and a battle against each other, for they both loved the same boy, Stesilaus of Ceos. The men were Themistocles and Aristides.

Themistocles grew up during the reign of Pisistratus. Pisistratus seized dictatorial power thanks to his influence over the poorer segments of the population. He was, in fact, the world's first known populist and as such popular. He did surprisingly well, putting Athens on the road to empire by taking certain islands and lands along the Hellespont, the most important being in Ionia on the western coast of today's Turkey. When he died his son Hippias, aided by his younger brother Hipparchus, took his place. The story of Hipparchus and that of the two lovers, Harmodius and Aristogeiton, have provided homophiles with one of the first ''modern'' homoerotic love stories, a story recounted with that of Achilles and Patroclus, Alexander and Hephaestion.

Hippias and Hipparchus were therefore joint dictators in Athens. Hipparchus fancied Harmodius who refused his advances. To gain revenge, Hipparchus refused to let Harmodius' sister take part in the Panathenaea Games, accusing her of not being a virgin, a requirement for the games. Harmodius and his lover Aristogeiton decided to rid Athens of the dictatorship and thusly redeem the honor of Harmodius' sister. With daggers hidden in their chitons, the boys fell on Hipparchus at the foot of the Acropolis, stabbing him to death. Hipparchus' guards immediately killed Harmodius, and Aristogeiton was captured. While being tortured to reveal any coconspirators, Aristogeiton agreed to tell the truth if Hippias would promise him clemency, sealed with a handshake. When Hippias complied, Aristogeiton laughed at his having shaken the hand of his own brother's murderer. Hippias, mad with fury, thrust his dagger into Aristogeiton's throat.

After the death of his brother, Hippias set up a more drastic form of dictatorship, becoming very unpopular, and was finally chased from power. Harmodius and Arostogeiton were declared liberators and countless statues were raised in their names. One statue was later captured by Xerxes who took it to Susa where Alexander the Great found it and returned it to Athens where it received divine honors. The legend of the two boys, and the sanctity of their love, was of such importance that even in Roman times statues of them continued to be sculpted. Their ancestors received vast privileges, such as free meals and front-row theater seats.

Alcibiades' family, the Alcmaeonids, in exile, felt that this would be a good time to return to Athens. They went to Delphi where, at immense expense, they had the sanctuary rebuilt. To thank them, the Oracle said to every delegation that came to Delphi: "I'll answer your questions, once Athens is free." This the Spartans, under the Spartan king Cleomenes, did by sending troops that blocked Hippias on the Acropolis. Hippias had sent his family away beforehand but the Spartans had captured them. To gain their freedom Hippias offered to give up his dictatorship, after which he fled to the court of Darius in Persia. When the Spartans learned that Cleomenes had swallowed the Oracle's oracle hook, line and sinker, they banished him. Cleomenes went to neighboring states and tried to raise an army against Sparta. To avoid this Sparta invited him back, but on arrival it was clear to them all that Cleomenes had become insane. He was thusly put away and Leonidas, of Thermopylae fame, took his place as king. Cleomenes then committed suicide by gnawing through his arms to his veins. Plutarch tells us that Cleomenes' beloved, Panteus, "the most beautiful and valorous youth in Sparta," killed himself out of faithfulness. Plutarch continues, "When he found Cleomenes lying motionless, he gave him a push and, seeing that he could still knit his brows, he kissed him, and raised him. Holding the body next to him, he plunged his sword into his own breast."

Some historians claim that Cleomenes' troubles originated from the fact that he was interested in what today we call foreign affairs, an interest other Spartans, highly conservation and content to remain in their boarders, found suspect: any man with such interests *had* to be insane. Then again, Cleomenes' interest had its limits. When the Ionian city-state of Miletus asked for the intervention of Sparta during the Ionian Revolt, promising Sparta fabulous riches when the Persian capital, Susa, was taken, Cleomenes gave his go-ahead. He withdrew it when he learned that the march from Miletus to Susa took three-months, an inconceivable distance. And finally, he may have gone insane due to his fondness for taking wine Scythian-style--unwatered. Polybius tells us that he was "a born ruler and king" and we learn from Plutarch that in his youth he was the beloved of the heartbreakingly handsome Xenares.

As Themistocles' mother was not Athenian, he was considered an outsider, but intelligently even as a child he persuaded well-born children to exercise with him, thusly breaking down the social barriers between them. Some say he was unruly and Plutarch informs us that one of his teachers told him, "One day you will be great, but whether for good or for evil only the future will tell." He was known for his love of boys but also for "honoring" his wife, as the French say, who produced numberous sons and daughters, one of which, his boy Neocles, died after being bitten by a horse. He also had his price. He reminds me of the story of Lincoln who received a bribe, in the presence of his son, a bribe he refused. The briber returned to the While House with a bribe twice as large, and again Lincoln, in the presence of his son, refused. When the man returned still later with three-times the last offer, Lincoln belted him. When the man left, Lincoln's son asked his father why he hadn't hit the man the first or the second time he attempted to bribe him. "Why did you hit him on the third visit only?" asked his boy. "Because on the third visit he came too close to my price." Themistocles would save Athens, but he too had his price.

Just before Themistocles rose to prominence, Cleisthenes took power. A democrat who introduced freedom of speech and action never known to the Athenians, he prepared the soil in which Themistocles grew to manhood. Cleisthenes introduced ostracism into Athens, something he hoped would reinforce democracy by allowing the Athenians, by a vote of 6,000 or more, to get rid of those they suspected of having tyrannical intentions. Themistocles would later misappropriate the system, using it to rid Athens and himself of his rival, Aristides, whose love for the boy they shared, Stesilaus, was becoming too invasive. But for the moment the reforms of Cleisthenes, says Plutarch, "allowed Athenians to become a great power by according them the greatest equality and freedom of speech any other country had ever achieved." Themistocles used the new freedom, Plutarch continues, "to become a first-class infighter, propagandist, always making himself visible to the people," a little like Alcibiades a few years later, but certainly without all of Alcibiades' rashness and seductive charm. Whereas one would always begin a description of Alcibiades as being beautiful, none of Themistocles' contemporaries ever did concerning him. Nonetheless, he "wooed the poor, courted the average Athenian in the taverns, on the docks and during his shopping in the markets. He canvassed as no politician before him, remembering the name of every man," says Plutarch. And the people supposedly loved him for it. He must have had a very common touch, because once any man rose even slightly above the masses, the Athenians, sooner or later, made him pay for it—often with his life.

The moment Themistocles gained power he put into movement the biggest ship building project in the history of Athens, making the country a major naval force, placing it directly on the path to empire. Thanks to Themistocles Athens became a cornucopia and Athenians benefited from all the goods known to the known world. The Piraeus, Athens' port, was expanded and the walls that would eventually connect the city with its port were begun. In all of this Themistocles set a course for Athens that has made Greece the immense sea power it is today.

Then came the invasion of Greece by the Persian Darius and Athens turned to a man older and more experienced than Themistocles, the general Miltiades. Thanks to his decisiveness Athenian forces marched to Marathon, accompanied by 1,000 Plataeans. They should have been accompanied by Spartans, but the Spartans didn't participate because the Persians' arrival fell during one of their religious festivities. Before the battle Miltiades called on the memory of the lovers Harmodius and Aristogeiton to inspire the troops, saluting them as "Athens' greatest heroes." The allies, a total of 10,000, engaged in a standoff against the Persians, numbering 20,000, until the Persian ships received a shield signal from a mysterious source beyond the beach, informing them that with Miltiades held down in Marathon, Athens itself was wide open. They therefore decided to cast anchor. Seeing this, Miltiades attacked from the surrounding hills. His combined army slaughtered the Persians still on the coast, many bogged down in the coastal marshes, killing, according to Herodotus, 6,400 of them. Miltiades lost 192 Athenians and Plataeans. The Athenians then ran back to Athens to warn the people of the arrival of the Persian fleet. When the enemy rounded Cape Sounion they saw the Athenians, in great numbers, coolly waiting to receive them. Darius gave orders to set sail for home.

The hallowed year of the Battle of Marathon was 490 B.C.

No one knows the name of the traitor who sent the shield signal to Darius. But it was certainly not the Spartans who, arriving too late, finally caught up with Athenians left to guard the beach at Marathon. The Spartans examined the dead Persians, kicking them as one does, today, a tire; they congratulated their Athenian comrades, patted them on the back, told them "well done", and then headed back to their mountain aerie.

Back in Athens Miltiades, after being so badly wounded in another campaign that he would soon die, was dishonored by Athenians who charged him with treason for having let his injury stop him from victory. He was sent to prison where he died of gangrene. The great sculptor Phidias erected a statue in his honor, dedicated to Nemesis, whose role it is to destroy those who become too mighty. Incredibly, it is said that the Persians themselves built a marble memorial to Miltiades, in memory of Marathon!

Themistocles moved in to fill the vacuum left by Miltiades, but the nobility of Athens, perhaps tired of Themistocles' plebian ways, decided to nominate Aristides, a man all knew to be virtuous, honest and incorruptible, to confront him. Aristides' followers called him "the just". Plutarch maintains that the rivalry between Aristides and Themistocles took a bitter turn due to their adoration of the same boy. In Plutarch's words, "They were rivals for the love of the beautiful Stesilaus of Ceos, and were passionate beyond all reason." The men fought over the boy by the intermediary of ships, Themistocles wanting more, Aristides wanting fewer. It ended in a close vote with the ostracism of Aristides, sent away from the city for ten years. Plutarch offers us a wonderful anecdote concerning what was, in reality, a referendum. An illiterate voter came up to Aristides whom he didn't know from sight and asked him to scratch the name of Aristides on the voting shard. When Aristides asked him how the man he was voting against had disappointed him, the voter replied, ''He didn't disappoint me but I'm sick and tired of hearing him always called 'the just.' '' Aristides duly inscribed his own name of the ballot.

The Persians returned, this time under Xerxes, at the head of 2,000,000 men, say some ancient historians. The Battle of Thermopylae took place, as described in the chapter on Leonidas.

After the battle, Xerxes entered Athens which Themistocles had ordered evacuated, except for a group of warriors entrenched on the Acropolis. They held out for two weeks before being massacred. Before leaving the city Themistocles had finally convinced the Spartans to fight at Salamis, threatening to withdraw Athenian ships, which made up half of the fleet, if they did not. Themistocles added that the Athenians would sail to the south of Italy where Greek colonies there claimed the land was a veritable horn of plenty.

Xerxes landed men on the island of Salamis, telling them to kill the Greeks who would swim there once the Persians had sunk their ships. The allied navy occupied the bay of Salamis. Themistocles wanted the Persians to enter the bay, knowing that their less maneuverable vessels would be at a disadvantage. To accomplish this, he sent his slave, Sicinnus, to the Persian camp to tell Xerxes that the Greeks, knowing they were outnumbered, would escape under darkness that night. He added that as the Athenians and Spartans hated each other, the Athenians had decided to go over to the great king's side. And in truth, this is what was happening. The Spartan Eurybiadas was in total disagreement with Themistocles, the reason the great Athenian sent his slave on such a perilous mission.

The Persians thusly entered the bay and, as foreseen, hindered by their number, they were boarded and their ships were set afire. Defeated and fearing that the Athenians would sail to the Hellespont and destroy the pontoon bridges, thusly blocking his retreat, Xerxes left, leaving his general Mardonius with the best troops to destroy what remained of the Greeks on the mainland. The Athenian general Aristides, recalled from exile, sailed to the island of Salamis and massacred the Persians who were in wait to massacre them.

Mardonius had numerous troops and might yet have won had the troops been reprovisioned. But with the ships fleeing with Xerxes, he was left dangling. He did wreck havoc. His forces attacked little Potidaea for three months until a tidal wave, the first in recorded history, destroyed their ships and drowned their men, saving Potidaea. The Spartans finally sent a huge force against Mardonius, but before meeting up with the Persians there was a total eclipse of the sun. Incredibly, unbelievably, the Spartans turned tail and headed home. Really, they never, ever, did anything like anyone else.

This, naturally, caused great stress between the Athenians and the Spartans. The Persian general Mardonius decided to take advantage of the dissention by asking King Alexander I of Macedonia to intervene (Alexander the Great was Alexander III). During the invasion by Darius Alexander had had the Persian ambassadors put to death, as did the Athenians and the Spartans. But now he was forced to help the Persians, although unknown to them he had also told the Athenians about Persian plans to attack Plataea in the north of Greece. Mardonius ordered Alexander to tell the Athenians that if they broke with Sparta the Persians would not only return all the territory they'd lost, but also reimburse them the costs of the war. Needless to say, the Athenians--after Sparta had abandoned them, first at Marathon, and now--were sorely temped to accept, but they knew that democracy was far better than Persian tyranny, even a benevolent tyranny under Xerxes. They therefore requested that the Spartans join them in sending troops to defend Plataea. At the same moment, the Athenians were obliged to flee from Athens a second time as a part of the Persian army took possession of it while the Athenians troops were away. Still again, the Spartans alleged a religious occurrence of some kind and refused to budge. The Athenians told them that in that case they would go over to the Persian side and invade the Peloponnesus. This riled the Spartans so much that they sent 5,000 men to join the Athenians, the largest body of troops ever to leave their country, accompanied by 5,000 perioeci, people living in Sparta but not citizens. The Athenians numbered 8,000 and there were 600 Plataeans, there to defend their homeland. The key to a victory would be Mardonius himself, known by all to be by far the most experienced military commander in Greece. So in the battle of Plataea it's not necessary to go into the details of "who entered from which angle" and precisions such as "the right wing was attacked while at the center..." etc. The only important fact is that Mardonius was killed with a spear through the chest. The Persians took flight the moment they learned of his death and the battle ended. Mardonius' corpse was respected by the troops but it later unaccountably disappeared. Of Mardonius' 120,000 men, 40,000 were thought to have escaped. The rest were slaughtered. Herodotus informs us that, in addition to Mardonius' death, the battle had been won thanks to the discipline and prowess of the Spartans, and this was certainly the case. Yet it was Athens that would reap the rewards and the honors, and it was now that Athens would rise to supreme power.

Afterwards the people only had eyes for Themistocles, but as I've said several times, the Athenians were insatiably jealous of their heroes, and in this Themistocles did not help himself for, like Alcibiades, he had the knack of making himself bigger than life. As Aristophanes put it, he farted higher than his ass. He was ostracized, an act which, says Plutarch, "was not a penalty but a way to pacify and alleviate jealousy, and humble the eminent." Taking no chances with his life, he fled, like Alcibiades years later, to Ionia. He went to the Persian throne of Artaxerxes. Both Plutarch and Thucydides tell us that Artaxerxes was thrilled to have an Athenian of such importance. Themistocles asked Artaxerxes for a year to learn the language and customs of Persia, after which he would serve him. This was granted. Although condemned to death in Athens, his family was able to escape and join him in exile. He lost his property but Artaxerxes awarded him the income from three Persian cities. According to Thucydides, he died of natural causes, but Plutarch claims that when the year was up, Artaxerxes ordered him to give the Persians aid in putting a definitive end to Athens. Refusing to finish his life dishonorably, he took poison and died. At any rate, he was 65. On his request, his bones were returned to Athens and secretly buried, some believe at the sight of the actual Athenian Naval Base.

Aristides died as he had lived, poor, honest and just.

And neither man got the boy. Stesilaus was, tragically, killed at Marathon.

CHAPTER SIX

LEONIDAS AND LOVE IN SPARTA

Leonidas was co-king of Sparta. There were always two kings, one of whom had to remain home when the other left on military or diplomatic adventures. Kingship passed from father to son, but only to sons born after his father had been named king. The kings were priests who solemnized sacrifices, and supreme commanders of the army. In the field they had absolute power of life and death, although they had nowhere near the power of Mycenaean Agamemnon. The historical reason for having two kings may be that their first king was followed, after his death, by his twin sons. Some recent historians suppose that the reason was to avoid absolutism, or perhaps points to a compromise between two adversarial families or communities. The kings were aided by a council of 28, whose members were age 60 or over. It was an oligarchy chosen by the people but only from the ranks of the nobility. There was an assembly of citizens over age 30 who could only debate proposals offered by the kings or ephors, and voted by acclamation. The ephors, five in number, represented the people and made sure the kings protected the people's interests. Anyone could be elected ephor. In this way there were near-perfect checks and balances: the kings checked each other; the council represented the nobility, and the assembly the people; and the ephors maintained correct rapport between the kings and their citizens. In time, only the kings and the ephors would count. Later still, it was the ephors who detained power, perhaps because the kings, competing against each other, were often in deadlock. Two ephors always accompanied the king who took the field. It was also they who decided foreign policy.

The southern part of the Peloponnese was divided in half by the Taygetus Mountains. The western section was extremely rich in comparison to the east, the home of the Spartans, and was known as Messenia, whose capital was Messene. Because the land was fertile and had a wonderfully wild climate, it was coveted and finally conquered by the Spartans who turned the inhabitants into helots. Helots had more rights than slaves because there was not a master to breathe down their necks. The Messenian lands had been divvied up among the Spartans, and the helots (Messenians) farmed them, giving the Spartans part of the produce and keeping the rest for their own survival. Helots could buy and own land. They weren't serfs exactly either in that any Spartan had the right to kill them (neither serfs nor slaves were ever murdered as were the helots, a phenomenon unique in world history), and part of a Spartan boy's training was exactly that, hunting down and murdering a helot. In a sense the helot was the boy's first ''man'', as today a boy downs his first deer. The Spartans murdered in reason, however, because not only were the helots needed to till the land, they also made up part of Spartan military forces, as well as being the baggage carriers and water boys. The helots were naturally dissatisfied with their lot, and ever eager to revolt. The simple fact is that if the Spartans hadn't trained themselves to become indomitable they would have been massacred in their sleep. The Spartans had a secret police, the Crypteia, that tried to choose likely helots for the boys' first kill. Plutarch's description is even more chilling: ''The boys would be supplied with daggers and at night if they came upon a helot they would cut his throat.'' Herodotus adds, ''When Spartans kill, they do so under the cover of night.'' The state's supremacy, therefore, was based on sudden death. A helot could be neither sold nor emancipated, except by the state itself. Under such draconian conditions, where the majority of the population consisted of hateful slaves, it's no wonder that the Spartans lived in perpetual uncertainty.

All of Sparta was a giant military camp. When a child was born it was washed in wine in the belief that this would fortify it. It was then examined. If found wanting, it was exposed on Mount Taygetus, in a chasm known as the apothetae. It was more common for boys than girls to be killed in this way, as boys had to be perfect. Trials for babies included bathing them in cold river water and exposing them to the elements, insuring that only the strongest would survive and procreate.

At age seven the survivors were trained to endure pain and hardships through incredibly difficult discipline, making them invincible and totally dedicated to the state. From the age of twelve they were watched over by older men who were their lovers, with whom they assuaged their passion where they could, outside the barracks. They were obliged to request this form of friendship, entering into it totally voluntarily.

The Spartans never hung around oil or perfume shops as did Alcibiades in Athens, but in their extremely limited lifespan, says Plutarch, ''They at times relaxed from the severity of their training or even, as at Thermopylae, during times of war. Then they beatified their hair and clothing, prancing around like horses, a true delight to the eyes.'' This was undoubtedly the great attraction for Alcibiades too.

The training center where the boys were enrolled at age seven was called the agoge (meaning ''rearing''). They lived in groups called herds, under the authority of whip-bearing older boys known as boy-herders. They were given a red cloak and told to make their beds out of reeds, pulled up by hand as they were not allowed knives, from the nearby Eurotas River (where Apollo lay with Hyacinth). They were underfed as an encouragement to go foraging--stealing--food to supplement their diet. There was no obesity under the Spartans, and thanks to this early training they could sustain hunger when on military campaigns. It appears that the sons of kings escaped this treatment. As said, they could enter a pedagogic relationship with older men at age twelve if they so chose. In these voluntary relationships the boys were sexually dominated, as older boys and men had to prove their strength and mastery in this practice (as they did in all others), a sexual bond that was both exceedingly intimate and yet known by all--there could be no secrets among companions who literally shared the same air. The boy was expected to endure the man's lust, although there were most probably moments of great tenderness among certain pairs. In exchange, the men made men of the boys, imparting that which was most precious to the boy, the men's knowledge. They learned enough math and reading to get by, and besides their daily training and hunting expeditions, they played ballgames and took up dancing and singing. At eighteen they became reserve members in the Spartan army and it was then that the best of them could join the Crypteia or secret police, their task being the spy on the helots. At age twenty they were voted into one of the messes by their peers, but all had to agree to their entry, a requisite that must have been an enormous incentive for them to prove themselves strong and loyal comrades at all times. Incredibly, they were allowed ten years during which they could attempt to be admitted into a mess; if they failed to do so they were denied Spartan citizenship. At age thirty they could marry. Childbearing was certainly limited by the fact that they married late and then had to sneak into the women's quarters to do their duty. As boys had only a slight degree of literacy, they were encouraged to develop their reading and oratorical skills if they become diplomats or generals later on.

In Athens and Sparta one had to be very careful in how one treated a citizen boy. There was a code that had to be respected before a lover could enter his beloved. The lover had to show himself worthy, valiant, protective, a good teacher in terms of knowledge and the handling of arms. Gifts were appreciated: a new cloak, a chiton, a cup, a sword, a dagger, perhaps even body armor. While awaiting the moment for the boy to give himself completely, sex was mutual manipulation and intercrural (between the thighs). The boy was never treated brusquely if a lover wanted him to agree to be his beloved. Things were totally different with women. They were bent over and entered from behind, vaginally and/or anally. They were also ordered on their knees while men thrust into their mouths, a scene on vases, but a scene not yet discovered concerning men (or men and boys). In intercrural sex men were painted on vases as, says Dover, ''bolt upright.'' An Athenian lost his manhood if he allowed himself to be entered, although some men certainly craved it, and what really took place in the shadows will always remain a mystery. Men who fuck a great deal are supposed to feel the difference between the vagina of a virgin and that of a woman fully broken it, between a vagina that has not known child birth and one that has, the reason why many Greeks preferred anal sex with woman, as it was simply tighter. Men seemed to have found it degrading to go down on other men in ancient times, and they never went down on women, an enormous contrast with today when fellatio is eagerly performed by women, and men seldom hesitate to return the favor.

The city-state was all-encompassing, and the people, as Plutarch says, ''hadn't the time to live for themselves but like bees they slaved away for the benefit of the whole community.'' The Spartans' had thusly engineered, arguably, the most extreme militaristic society in recorded history.

Women were trained like boys and were noted for their chastity. Because they had to defend the city-state when the men were away, they were, paradoxically, better educated and better fed than other women in the Greek world, especially when compared to Athens that treated its women with Persian-style misogynic disregard. Athenian women were there to cook and to bring forth boys. They were in the custody of their husbands, legally minors. A man caught having sex with them or any other woman in the household could be killed on the spot with total immunity. As men married in their late thirties and women married virgin when they were around 15, boys looked for sex among themselves. So at the age when girls were losing their virginity, boys were too. It must be remembered that at the time, puberty set in much later than today. Even during the Renaissance boys of 15 were often prepubescent. As puberty was late, one wonders if sex occurred with those boys who hadn't even their very first pubic hairs. According to many sources boys weren't supposed to have pleasure during intercourse, in which case their being old enough to have an orgasm and/or emit semen is unimportant. Yet it's difficult to believe that boys in ancient Sparta or Athens—whom men genuinely adored—could have been treated so callously.

If Spartan women couldn't produce offspring with their husbands, they bred for their country by being serviced by studs known for the fecundity of their seed. Husbands fully accepted this because they understood that they had to produce boys who would someday stand for them when they entered a room, as they now stood for their leaders.

Most of what we know about Sparta (and it's incredibly confused and limited) comes through Xenophon who sent his sons there to be educated much as, today, a father sends his boys to a military academy in the hopes that it will straighten them out. A Spartan boy had his admirers, who were many, and his lover, who was unique and with whom he exchanged emotive pledges. Nature being what it is, a boy may have wound up having many lovers, one at a time, and a lover many boys—*perhaps* one at a time. The boy then grew to become a man and took a boy, and the eternal cycle was repeated. It was good for a boy to have as many admirers as possible, good for his ego and for his future place in society, as each admirer would place a stone in the construction of the boy's ascendancy (it was good for his father's status too). The criteria were a beautiful face and a beautifully made body, but these were often ephemeral in comparison to a boy's courage, intelligence, personality, charisma and general lovability—not to mention his or his family's wealth and social status.

The boys crept out of their barracks to have intercourse with their wives, the stealthy stealing into the night firing the lust of their young, healthy loins, insuring the powerful inseminations that would bring forth sons of their own (and who would one day, it has to be repeated, rise to their feet for them, as they now rose for their feet for their current commanders). The girls were said to have had shaved heads and to have worn cloaks like the boys. Their husbands slipped into their cots at night and left nearly immediately to return to the barracks and their companions. Plutarch says that in many cases the men even had children before seeing what their wives looked like in daylight! It's highly possible that this exceptional way of lovemaking--charging around in the dead of night like thieves--had been decided on in order to charge a boy's sexual libido to the maximum. Once they had children, Spartans could continue in this way or set up housekeeping in homes of their own. Sparta was a wild country, full of trees, bushes, ferns, boulders, brooks, meadows and mountains, all of which provided veils in acts of love and passion, although the usual sites for trysts between men and boys were just outside the barracks, gymnasia, training fields and campsites. As noted, a man too old to reproduce was obliged by law to get a young man whom he admired to do for his wife what he couldn't.

Men could impregnate boys but one had to be discreet about it. The tyrant Periander was murdered because during a drinking bout he asked his beloved, in front of numerous friends, whether by this time in their friendship the boy was not yet with child. The boy leaned over as if fiddling with his sandals, and when his lover bent to see what he was doing, he thrust his knife into his lover's chest. When word spread as to the reason he had acted as he did, he got off with the approbation of his peers, the other boys.

Xenophon goes on to describe a tender battle scene in which a certain Episthenes, seeing that a handsome enemy boy was about to be executed, ran to Xenophon and begged for the boy's life. Xenophon approached his general, Seuthes, in charge of Episthenes, to ask if the lad's life could be spared, as Episthenes had shown himself a valiant warrior. Seuthes asked Episthenes if he would be willing to take the boy's place and be executed. Episthens stretched out his neck and told Seuthes to strike off his head if the boy so ordered. The boy came forward to save Episthenes, but dropped to his knees and begged that both their lives be spared. Episthenes rose and enfolded the lad in his arms, telling Seuthes that he would have to kill them or let them both go free. Seuthes laughed and, says Xenophon, winked at him.

The story is certainly true as someone of Xenophon's value would never have recounted it otherwise, but one nonetheless wonders how many other boys have been senselessly sacrificed through other countless, senseless wars. (Sorry, I immediately get teary where the survival of boys is concerned. I'll never digest the murder of 8,000 Bosnians, from age 13, who certainly begged to be spared until the last heartrending second.)

A Spartan had no life of his own; he had no existential problems to solve. Who knows? Perhaps there was something satisfying in the comradeship among men, knowing that when one awoke his day was planned, that he and his friends would eat, train and exercise together, march, sing and laugh in the fullness of men raised as brothers. Nothing to question; nothing to fear as long as they remained united. A visitor to their country must have been very surprised: an unwalled city of men and women who chose a healthy existence, one of bravery and simplicity, who followed the Apollonian ideal of moderation in all things.

Theognis, who at times complains, in his poetry, of his own lover who is often fickle and promiscuous, suggests there were nevertheless other rewards:

Happy the lover who exercises, then
Goes home to sleep all day with a handsome boy.

At first Leonidas' mother didn't produce children. Her husband was therefore allowed to have a second wife, from whom came Cleomenes. The first wife then gave birth to a boy, followed by Leonidas. The children of Spartan kings who were eligible for the throne did not have to pass through the rigorous schooling of other Spartan boys. But because Leonidas was not considered as a possible heir to kingship, he was forced to go through the agoge like the other herds, a task which greatly hardened him and supremely prepared him for war. Then one brother died in Africa, another was declared insane and fled Sparta. Leonidas then came to power, one of the best-trained kings in Spartan history. He was thusly chosen to lead 300 of Sparta's finest against Xerxes as Thermopylae. Spartan friendships being what they were, Leonidas knew he could count on every man. But as additional assurance, for the 300 he chose, exclusively, men and boys who had taken vows as lovers and beloveds.

The Spartans were convinced that Xerxes could be stopped at the hot sulfur springs called Thermopylae. This was a narrow pass between the sea and the mountains the Persians would be forced to take. King Leonidas went there at the head of the 300, as well as the forces of other allies. Sadly, the Spartans sent no more than the 300 because they were not interested in protecting Attica. They wanted to stop the Persians at the Isthmus of Corinth, thereby sparing the Peloponnese. Despite the confidence of the Spartans back home, Leonidas knew it was a suicide mission, and when one of his friends murmured that the Persians would be so numerous that their arrows would block out the sun, Leonidas answered, ''Then we'll fight in the shade.'' Leonidas had also been chosen by the Spartans who knew that other nations would send troops thanks to his reputation of always winning; none—or few—would therefore medize.

Before leaving Sparta Leonidas sent to Delphi to learn what the Oracle had to say about the coming conflict. To say the least, the Oracle was, this time, precise:

> To you, courageous and brave men of beautiful Sparta,
> Either your glorious city will be wasted by Persians,
> Or you will mourn your greatest king, from Heracles' line.

Xerxes' spies reported to him that the Spartans were exercising, bathing in the sea and caring for their hair. He asked the Spartan renegade Demaratus what was going on. On arriving at Xerxes' court Demaratus had been given rule over certain Persian towns, rule that was destined to continue, through his descendants, for centuries. He now told the king that this was the Spartan way to prepare for death. When the king asked for more, Demaratus went on to tell the king that the Spartan army was the greatest the world had ever known, for they were free men fighting freely. Demaratus then said that the law was Sparta's only master, from which we have the incredibly moving Spartan epitaph known to every schoolboy, raised to honor the 300: *Go tell the Spartans, stranger passing by, that here, obedient to Spartan law, we lie*. When Xerxes said that this was ridiculous, Damaratus bowed low and said he'd spoken only because the king had desired him to do so, but from then on he would remain silent, adding that he hoped that all would go as the king wished.

The Persians held back, certain that the Spartans, seeing the enormous number of enemy troops, would end up fleeing, despite Damaratus' warning. Xerxes sent an embassy to Leonidas, telling him that if he gave up the fight Xerxes would make him king of all of Greece. Leonidas answered that if the Persians had an iota of the true values in life, they would not covet what belonged to others. When the ambassadors again urged him to give up his arms, he answered, "Come and get them yourselves!" It was only on the fifth day that they finally attacked. Xerxes lost 20,000 men, among them many of Xerxes' elite troops, the Immortals. Spartans and their allies lost 2,500. The Persians withdrew to lick their wounds.

In fact they held back until Leonidas was betrayed by a local, Ephialtes, who led the Persians along a mountain track that outflanked the Spartans. Aware of what was happening, Leonidas dismissed the greater part of his troops and covered their escape with a force of 2,000, 300 Spartans, 900 helots and 700 Thespians from a town in Boeotia that Xerxes later destroyed in reprisal. All the Spartans were massacred after killing as many Persians as they could. There are several theories as to why Leonidas sent the other troops away. Perhaps he thought he had to fulfill the Oracle from Delphi, or perhaps he wanted to save the men so that they could fight another day. Perhaps, some say, he knew that the men he dismissed didn't have the heart to fight to the death, and by dismissing them the Battle of Thermopylae would live on in the memory of free men as one of the most glorious pages in Spartan history—which is precisely what occurred. The Persians, still afraid of the Spartans and their remaining allies, shot thousands of arrows from a safe distance into the enemy ranks, killing them off one by one. When Leonidas fell, his men covered his body with their cloaks. When they too died, Xerxes had Leonidas beheaded and his body hung from a stake. The Persian troops then continued on to Athens, short of two of Xerxes' brothers who had been killed at Thermopylae, while their ships sailed to the final countdown at Salamis. The Spartans hid behind the wall they built across the Isthmus of Corinth, leaving Athens--from which the Athenians fled to the island of Salamis--to be razed by the Persians.

The hallowed year of the Battle of Thermopylae was 480 B.C.

CHAPTER SEVEN

ALCIBIADES

The world loves a rogue, and there is no better example than Alcibiades. He was all things to those who crossed his path: intelligent, courageous, ambitious, eloquent in speech, charm personified, so handsome that it's the first adjective employed by biographers and historians alike, sexually versatile, the ideal top to women, the perfect bottom to men; he was totally amoral, as depraved as a teenager, as corrupt as a cop, as streetwise as a delinquent, as pampered as the son of a wallstreeter, as sexy as Paul Newman; he was irreligious, treasonous, and the proof that the gods really do raise to dizzying heights those they wish to utterly destroy.

Today we have showmen, great orators, warriors and boys who are totally fearless. We have boys who are nearly superhuman in their beauty. There are arrogant boys, willful boys and, naturally, boys who's only interest is in themselves. There are lusty boys who live for sex, taking bodies and offering their own; boys who get off with girls, and boys who go with other boys or other boys and girls. But never have we had a combination of all these things as we have in Alcibiades.

He sought ways to remain in the public eye, going so far as to cut off the tail of his dog, its most beautiful attribute. This caused the desired scandal among the Athenians to which he answered, ''Well, I got the attention I was looking for on the one hand, while taking their attention away from the really bad things I've been up to.''

Many men were thought to have slept with him as a boy. Once, when he disappeared for over a week, Pericles' friends suggested that an alarm should be raised in order to find him. Pericles had been named the boy's guardian since the death of his father when the boy was ten. He now answered that if the lad were dead a general alarm would only find him a little earlier than if there were no alarm at all; if he were alive, on the other hand, the discovery that he had run away would only harm his reputation. Left unsaid was the certainty that if he had run away it was certainly with some man, as no woman could supply him--or would dare supply him--with the luxuries to which he was accustomed. When Alcibiades found out that his guardian, the most respected man in Athens, had defended him, he knew that from then on he could do exactly as he wished. ''For now on,'' he said to his companions, ''the Athenians can kiss my royal ass.''

Anytus, a rich lad, was very found of him and invited Alcibiades to a meal among friends. Alcibiades arrived with companions but proceeded only to the dining room doorway from which he greeted Anytus and his guests, seated before a table with silver and gold tableware. Anytus was, asserts Athenaeus (who goes out of his way to do so), ''Alcibiades' lover.'' Alcibiades ordered his companions to gather up half of the tableware, after which he bade Anytus a good evening. When Anytus' friends, scandalized, asked what Anytus was going to do about the theft Anytus answered that, on the contrary, Alcibiades had shown great tenderness in not taking it all.

As hope springs eternal in the human breast, Anytus certainly expected that Alcibiades would show other forms of tenderness at another time.

Alcibiades received gifts (or took gifts, as he did at Anytus' dinner) in exchange for love, the penalty for which, at certain times in Athens, was death. Athenian citizens could sell their bodies to whom they wished, but in doing so they could no longer benefit from the rights accorded to citizens. They could no longer speak before the Assembly. They could no longer use the courts for reparation should they in anyway be maligned. If they attempted to do so, they were in real danger of being stoned to death. All that was needed was for someone, anyway, to prove that the person had, at any time in his life, sold himself. A foreigner, on the other hand, someone who was not an Athenian citizen, could prostitute himself/herself without any juridical consequences of any sort. Many foreigners did so and perhaps the totality of male Athenians took advantage of their services at one time or another. When the boy Alcibiades left his bedroom at Pericles' home, it was to sleep with a man who had something to offer him, and the "something" in question was often money. Alcibiades, as a youth, was a high-class rent-boy who escaped punishment thanks to his guardian, Pericles.

Handsome lads were in great demand in Athens and as the competition to win their favors was fierce, it often cost their aspirants a small fortune, not to speak of the lengthy wooing. Life wasn't always easy for the boys either, as they couldn't show themselves as being too easy for fear of being treated as whores. Stringent laws tried to protect them, but it was clear that when boys wanted to amuse themselves, total surveillance was next to impossible. Foreigners and slaves could be put to death if they tried their hand at boy-love with Athenian citizens. Stringent punishment was reserved for teachers and trainers who had access to them in schools and gymnasiums, access forbidden to older boys over eighteen. Their fathers' male friends were especially carefully watched. If a guardian prostituted the boy he was supposed to protect, he could be stoned. If men couldn't get what they wanted from "nice" boys, there were always whorehouses. They flourished throughout Athens. The ones for boys had courts where the lads sunned themselves, naked, their wares in varying states of arousal. But whorehouses offered compensations. With "nice" boys, men often had to content themselves with intercrural sex, performed upright with the penis inserted between the thighs, while in whorehouses they could penetrate anally to their hearts' content. They could also get blown, otherwise a seemingly rare occurrence in antiquity. (The practice is so common today that I hesitate to be too definitive!)

Cruising areas were the market place, back streets, in the martial arts schools, in cemeteries, along the quays of the Piraeus and in the Ciramicus, the potters' quarter, northwest of the Acropolis. Sex was mostly a hidden activity, although some amphorae and twin-handled cups show men fucking in full view of other men, leaving one to wonder just how private a matter sex was, under certain circumstances, in ancient times.

Philemon tells us that the great lawgiver Solon, seeing that young men at times did very unlawful and foolish things due to their inability to find a sexual outlet, allowed prostitutes, male and female, to post themselves throughout Athens in front of their housing, totally naked so as not to fool the client. One paid one's obol and took one's pleasure. A person who sold himself could be used by the client in any way he wished, which is the definition of hubris, and therefore against Athenian law. This means that there was a lot of looking-the-other-way when it benefited the general population.

Love between men has rarely been a long tranquil river. At times lovers fought, sword in hand, for the love of a boy. Plutarch tells us of Theron who chopped off his own thumb to show his love for his beloved, and challenged a rival to do the same. Plutarch mentions, too, the case of Konon who killed himself, weary of the tasks imposed on him and never rewarded by a youth he wished to have as a beloved.

Alcibiades had the image of Eros embossed on his shield that Athenaeus states was made of ivory and gold, leaving no doubt as to his amorous pretentions, to the loathing of virtuous Athenians. Having been brought up in the company of the likes of his guardian, Pericles, and Pericles' friends--actors, statesmen, philosophers, as well as the whores Pericles frequented--there was little that the boy didn't know and hadn't experienced from a very young age. The philosopher Bion suggests that he had indeed begun early on: ''Even as a child he made men unfaithful to their wives, and as a young man he made women unfaithful to their husbands.'' Aristophanes tells us in *The Frogs*, ''They love him and hate him, but cannot do without him.'' He wrote another play, lost, entitled *The Man with Three Dicks,* in which Alcibiades' erotic exploits were satirized. Alas, we know not in what way.

Statues of Hermes, god of travelers, were erected at crossroads. Their particularity was a fully engorged phallus with ample foreskin. As crossroads were places of encounter, the phalli took on erotic signification. Boys looking for adventure would stroke them for luck, girls searching for husbands did likewise, and women wanting children made pilgrimages to the sites—in fact, the phalli were polished to a luster. During the night preceding an expedition to capture Sicily, Hermes' phalli throughout Athens were vandalized, most probably by drunken pranksters, exactly the milieu frequented--and most often led--by Alcibiades, a youth known by all for his brilliant intellect and total absence of morality. As during our own times, in ancient Athens too people were unduly respectful of those of high birth and affluence, the reason they were reluctant to attack Alcibiades head on. The destruction was also heresy, as Hermes was an Olympian god. And it was the worst possible omen prior to a military enterprise. But there was a strong possibility that Alcibiades would escape punishment thanks to his connection with Pericles and his immense wealth.

The problem with Sicily began in 415 B.C.--the 17th year of the Peloponnesian war--when a delegation from the island came to tell Athenians that the time was ripe for them to conquer Syracuse, the most important city-state on Sicily. The peoples of Syracuse were ethnical Dorians, as were the Spartans, whereas the members of the delegation from the much smaller city-state of Segesta were ethnical Ionians, like the Athenians. Syracuse, the island's principal city, was about the size of Athens. It was rich and the island richer. Its capture would supply Athens with immense wealth, resources and more wheat than Athens would ever need. Sicily was the breadbasket of the Greek world, as, later, Egypt would be for the Romans.

Alcibiades wanted to go to war and soon he had the Athenians on their knees, drawing sketches of the island in the sand, each vying to place the major island towns in their right places. Men and boys were forming lines to join up as members of the expedition, certain that they would reap gold through sacking the palaces and homes of the rich inhabitants. The delegation from Segesta arrived with 60 talents of silver (a talent weighed 26 kilos) and plates of solid gold. In addition, they declared that their temples and citizens possessed a treasure in solid gold vessels. The Athenians sent a delegation to assure itself that this was so; the members returned with smiles on their faces. This turned the heads of the Athenians, and especially that of the handsome Alcibiades who was always in deed of lucre.

When the Athenian noble Nicias saw that Alcibiades had stirred up the blood of Athenians hungry for war and the riches reaped through war, he threw in his support, so long as he was named general and the size of the fleet and the number of warriors involved in Alcibiades' plan were at the very least doubled, thereby giving Athens a chance at success. He did warn his friends, however, to beware of Alcibiades who would one day endanger Athens in order to live a brilliant life of his own.

When the full Athenian force did finally arrive in Sicily, it discovered that the solid gold brought to Athens by the Segestaeans was only silver plated with gold, and the solid gold vessels the expedition had seen at Segesta had only been the same vessels passed from house to house and from temple to temple!

Alcibiades wanted to be judged for the crime against Hermes before setting sail for Sicily, aware that during his absence his enemies, were he not judged, would do what was necessary to turn heads and buy votes. After all, the penalty for heresy was death. Athenians were as serious about offending the gods as were Europeans, later, under the Inquisition. Had his request to be judged before setting sail been accepted, he would have certainly been acquitted for the simple reason that the Athenians needed him for their intervention. But the request was refused, and he prepared to leave for Sicily as co-general with Nicias at the head of what Thucydides said was the greatest armada ever raised by a single Greek state, 134 triremes and a far greater number of smaller ships, as well as 30,000 men. Diodorus Siculus recounts that all of Athens--inhabitants, friends, lovers and children--traipsed behind the warriors as they made their way to the Piraeus, singing and waving fronds. The ships bobbing in the harbor had been fully decked out with banners, flags and pennants, their sides covered with the shields of all the participating countries, those furnishing soldiers or money. Perfume burners and fires in bronze vessels consumed incense in such quantity that the air was misty with it. Lovers kissed their friends goodbye and the boys went off to their fates

Just after arrival at the island of Sicily, a ship, the *Salaminia*, came from Athens demanding that Alcibiades return to stand trial for the destruction of the Hermes' statues. Judging from the behavior of the emissaries sent to bring him back, Alcibiades knew what awaited him at home. He knew that the Athenians had perfected the art of using men for their own benefit, but that they would then humble and chasten them when the men became too powerful or too well known. This was a highly dangerous move on the part of the Athenians because the army and sailors favored Alcibiades, who had an uncanny way of winning over the men under his command; the Athenians therefore treated him with kid gloves, promising anything to get him aboard. Otherwise, they knew, the whole army would mutiny. Besides the army's love for him, the soldiers also felt that under someone indecisive like Nicias the war could drag on for an eternity, with no riches, as Alcibiades had promised, at the end. Alcibiades agreed to return but on his own ship.

Unknown to all, his true destination was Sparta. A Spartan nurse had cared for Alcibiades and had instilled the love of Sparta in the child's heart. Also, his family had had traditional connections with Sparta. When a Spartan delegation came to Athens in search of a peace agreement in 421 Alcibiades, thanks to his family, enjoyed privileged access to the ephors. Alcibiades didn't waste time in seducing the Spartans. He wore their coarse clothes, bathed in cold water, ate their disgusting broths, drank their inferior wines, and fucked their women, one of whom was King Agis' wife who bore Alcibiades' son Leotychides. Alcibiades counted on Leotychides to found a new Spartan race of Alcibiadesian origin. It didn't help matters much when Agis' wife went around calling her baby Alcibiades, the name she preferred to Leotychides. Alcibiades could play the role of the perfect Spartan, Plutarch tells us, because he was the perfect chameleon--all things to all men, displaying virtue or vice as the occasion called. It must have been marvelous to observe his technique because men really liked and appreciated him, and being a man's man is not an easy task. Plutarch goes on to say that in Sparta he devoted himself to athletic exercises; in Ionia he enjoyed the luxury of the baths, oiled and perfumed, at ease with the fondling of both sexes; in Thrace he drank to the dregs among the dregs; in Thessaly he awed all with his horsemanship; and in Persia he exceeded even the Persians in magnificence. He was thusly accused of playing a double game, but men have been known to willfully march to more than just one tune without having treacherous motives.

Alcibiades' sex with Spartan men would have been rapid and carnal, but with a Spartan boy he would have taken advantage of a hunting expedition when, sheltered probably by a rocky outcropping, he would have lain alongside the lad, both enrobed in the traditional wine-red Spartan cloak. He would have pressed his cloth-enclosed erection against the other's buttocks, perhaps occasionally reaching around to caress the lad through the folds of wool. At no time would skin come into contact with skin. Alcibiades would have ejaculated in this way, into the fabric. The boy too would have ejaculated thanks to the pushing of his penis against the tissue and rocky surface, or he would have brought himself off with his own hand, hidden in the folds of his own cloak. In this way historians have attempted to bring understanding to the multiple texts on the subject, each vague and contradictory, about how men had sex with young boys they called striplings. As usual with Sparta, nothing was ever clear-cut.

Alcibiades had been sentenced to death when he hadn't returned to Athens, and now he was again sentenced to death, this time by the cuckolded Agis. It seems that Agis had no difficulty in believing the rumors of his wife's unfaithfulness simply because for a period of ten months that followed an earthquake--the magnitude of which had scared him out of his wits while copulating with her--he hadn't dared approach her again. Leotychides had been conceived during this time. Luckily Alcibiades was forewarned, giving him an opportunity to flee to his supreme enemy's camp: the Persian Tissaphernes.

Tissaphernes was the governor (called a satrap) of the western part of Phrygia, Lydia and Caria, a diplomat, a general and a key advisor to King Darius II. And he was right up Alcibiades' alley in the sense that he too was a lover of guile, an admirer of rogues, as well as being wonderfully subtle. He was also 40, an age during which a man especially appreciates a boy's beauty. And there was no one more beautiful and intelligent than Alcibiades, possessor of behavior so smooth it anesthetized the Persians into believing everything he said. In fact, Tissaphernes named his most beautiful garden, containing streams and meadows, pavilions and baths, Alcibiades Park, the name it was referred to ever after, a pleasure retreat both men shared during Alcibiades' sojourn. The situation was indeed remarkable as Tissaphernes loathed the Greeks for the disaster they wrought on Darius I and Xerxes. He was also, Plutarch says, psychopathic and perverse. Yet he ended up flattering Alcibiades even more than Alcibiades—an expert—flattered him. Thucydides wrote that the real reason for Alcibiades' treason was the hope that the Athenians would, in desperation, recall him.

And this was a possibility as things were going very wrong for Athens. Inaction on the part of Nicias and his advisors gave the Sicilians time to build more ships and rearm. They were not accomplished sailors, far less so than the Athenians, but they were fighting for their lives and survival as a people, an incredibly strong incentive. During a first naval battle at Plemmyrion, a harbor very chose to Syracuse, the Athenians fought in a restricted space unfit for their large vessels but perfect for Syracuse's smaller ships. Reinforcements promised by Athens arrived late, held up by storms, after the Syracusans had inflicted great damage. Athenian land forces then tried to capture a Syracusan fort atop a cliff overlooking the harbor. When this failed the attackers tried to withdraw, which caused panic among those still climbing upwards. Men lost their footing and attempted to cling to what they could after flinging away their spears and shields. Most fell to their deaths, a reported 2,000 in all.

Nicias met with his advisers who all advised withdrawal back to Greece. But Nicias, perhaps fearful of the consequences when he confronted the citizens of Athens, perhaps suffering from the Trojan complex--he and his men called women as the Trojans had been when they lost their city--decided to carry on. Alas, no one had the authority to stop him. He did decide, however, to abandon the Plemmyrion harbor. But before he could, an external event made him change his mind, which is sad because had he done so, he would have escaped with his life and ships. But Nicias was a superstitious man who believed in signs and omens. One such sign was a full eclipse of the moon, an omen that seemed to indicate that he should remain where he was. This gave the Syracusans time to block the entrance of the harbor with every ship and floating vessel at their disposal, all linked by heavy chains. On the hills surrounding the harbor local villagers turned out to watch from an incomparable bird's-eye view. Over the days that followed they saw one side win the battle, only to be undone on the next day; the Athenians on board the ships cried victory one moment, while moaning their defeat the next. In the end the Athenians abandoned their ships in favor of an escape overland. But again Nicias changed his mind. This too was sad because historians believe that had they set off immediately, Nicias and his men would have been able to make their way, on foot, to Sicilian colonies that were still in their corner. But Syracusan spies infiltrated Nicias' ranks, telling the soldiers that the roads leading away from the harbor were blocked, and that they would do well to prepare themselves before confronting the enemy. This they believed and remained a day too long, the time needed for the Syracusans to really block the passages out. The Athenians had thusly to fight their way through the enemy, which caused damage in the ranks, but the worst destruction was reserved for laggards, consisting of the weak, the wounded and the sick. As usual on the battlefield, dysentery was a mortal enemy, emptying the body of its substance in the most despicable fashion known to men.

Nicias finally sued for peace, offering to pay the stupendous sum of a talent per man spared, a sum that would be guaranteed by Athens, putting the city-state in debt for years to come. The Syracusans refused, and the Athenians continued their death march. Hungry and dying of thirst, they made their way to the river Assinaros, one that would have a dreaded reputation for all time. Here the Athenians literally climbed over each other to gain access to the stream, while Syracusans, catching up with them on horseback, slaughtered them with arrows and spears from the banks, but even then the men drank water muddy and red with blood. The survivors were rounded up and sold into slavery, most of whom were sent to stone quarries where they disappeared from history. The lucky ones, those who were handsome, were handed over as sexual slaves, and there is at least a chance that they were well treated. Nicias, whom the Syracusans held responsible for the misery and death of so many Sicilian warriors, was tortured in the most miserable fashion, says Thucydides without going into detail, before his throat was slit. The Syracusans had been forced to fight for their survival, and as such must certainly not be blamed for wanting to keep their freedom. So content were they that from then on, each and every year, they organized festivities in honor of their victory, festivities known as the Assinarian Games.

Back in Athens the women went on the world's first sex strike, hoping to force the men to make peace before making love. But Greece being Greece (at that time, at least), this was hardly a hardship. There's an anecdote that comes down to us through a play by Aristophanes, *Lysistrata*. One of the women in the play, who had taken part in the sex strike, now complained about how impossible it was to get sex once a woman was old: "It's the same with men," a man answers. "Not at all," the woman continues. "Any grey-haired man can pick up a young girl, but a woman's season is short." (She didn't foresee the advent of cougars.)

It was at this moment that Alcibiades chose to reenter the scene. He sent negotiators to Samos to inform the Athenians stationed there with their fleet that he could arrange an alliance with Tissaphernes who was at the moment in favor of the Spartans. But Tissaphernes wanted an end to Athenian democracy, favoring an oligarchy headed by Alcibiades--whom Tissaphernes trusted--instead. The Athenian population on the island, believing themselves to be every bit as qualified to represent Athenians as were the Athenians in Athens, decided to forgive Alcibiades--with, perhaps, the ulterior motive that he would still be able to bring Tissaphernes over to their side, a sentiment that Alcibiades encouraged. The Athenian general Thrasybulus, stationed at Samos, was sent to bring Alcibiades to Samos where he was made general. The island was known for its beautiful boys, one of whom was sought out by all generals and politicians passing by. He was Bathylle and the poet Anacreon had his portrait painted, giving these instructions to the artist: ''And between his charming, incendiary thighs, paint a noble member that aspires to be loved.''

The men on Samos adored Alcibiades as he had been adored wherever he set foot. Right off the bat he won a series of victories so grand that the soldiers and sailors felt exalted and glorified. And Plutarch goes on: ''The army directly under him felt so superior to the other soldiers that they wouldn't mix with them.'' He added that, ''While others had known defeat, Alcibiades' men were invincible.'' Although Thrasybulus was responsible for many victories, ''it was always Alcibiades,'' says Cornelius Nepos, ''not Thrasybulus, who reaped the glory, thanks to his golden rhetoric and natural gifts.'' Luckily, a little later Alcibiades' superheroes found themselves in difficulty during another battle, and were saved by the rabble soldiers they had thumbed their noses at. The result was that they all kissed and made up, and had a huge barbeque during which bread and meat were thrown around, from one man to another, as a sign of friendship.

As general, Alcibiades led his ships into the Hellespont to gather money and sailors. He went from victory to victory, doing wonders for Athenian morale. Soon Alcibiades was Athens' uncontested leader. Before he personally returned to his homeland he sent his troops into the city to tell of his glorious victories, thereby assuring his triumphal arrival. Only then did he bring captured Spartan galleys into the Piraeus, loaded with spoils, bedecked with dancers, lyre players and drummers, his own ships rigged with his signature purple sails--the indisputable hero of his people. He made his way to the Acropolis through throngs of delirious well-wishers. Cornelius Nepos goes on to tell us that he gave a speech in which he blamed the Fates for his troubles, and not the Athenians, now shedding tears, who had nonetheless sentenced him to death. (The hypocrisy was, of course, mindboggling, but as usual he knew exactly what he was doing.) He emphasized the fact that he had influence over Tissaphernes who promised, said Alcibiades, to make sure that Athens and Athenians never lacked for food or money, even if it meant that he, Tissapernes, ''ended up selling his own bed.'' He was applauded, his estates were returned, and priests annulled the curses aimed at him. From here on the Athenians went from victory to victory until the entire Hellespont was theirs. Alcibiades was given complete charge over the war and carte blanche in any attempt to come to terms with Persia. But victory is an unfaithful mistress.

Alcibiades returned to Samos and tried to engage the Spartans, but they were too wary of his power. They bided their time until he went off to the Hellespont to gather money and additional soldiers. The Spartan navy chose that moment to strike and win a series of battles. Alcibiades lost the backing of Athens, and rather than lose his life too, he retreated to a castle in Thrace that he had had the forethought to construct. The Athenians still outnumbered the Spartans in ships and tried to engage them in the Hellespont, in view of Alcibiades' fortification. The Athenians anchored in the harbor of Lampsacus, the Spartans at Aegospotami. Soon a daily routine set in. Day after day the Athenians would sail from Lampsacus to Aegospotami, but the Spartans always refused to leave their protective harbor to fight. The Athenians would then sail back to Lampsacus where they would disembark for a leisurely meal on the shore and horse around as boys and men are like to do at the beach. One day Alcibiades left his lair and came down to warn the leaders that they should be more on the lookout, and the army far more disciplined. The Athenians gazed on Alcibiades, atop his horse, his purple robe open to the navel, his skin oiled, his hair and beard carefully curled, and shook their heads in wonder at this man who had lorded it over Athens since his childhood, and who was now in self exile. Some knew him, some knew him even very well. For them all, this was just Alcibiades being Alcibiades. They thanked him because it was conceivable that he would live to reign again over them all. He rode away, his long robe spread over the horse's ass.

When the Spartans felt that the time was ripe, they set sail for Aegospotami where they attacked the Athenian forces, asleep in the shade of the afternoon sun. There was no battle. The men on shore scurried into the hinterland and those on the ships surrendered. Of the 180 vessels present, only 20 got away. Four thousand boys and men, then and there, had their throats cut, depriving them of their lust and their beauty and their already much-to-short lives.

Alcibiades, who had been deified a few short months before by the Athenians, was now, after the defeat, vilified for his arrogance and general depravity. The people knew about his castle on the Hellespont and hated him for it, wondering why such a fortification had been deemed necessary and how much of Athens' treasury its walls protected. The castle was located in Thrace, a land known for its barbarians. There, Alcibiades had his own private army which he used to despoil his neighbors. Cornelius Nepos tells us that, as in all the other countries Alcibiades had lived, in Thrace too he had seduced the local louts, drinking them under the table and screwing among what Thracians considered their nobility, as well as among the dregs. But as there is no honor among thieves, as soon as the Thracian brigands learned that the Athenians and the Spartans were set on Alcibiades' death, they began to plunder his wealth, daring him to do anything about it. He fled into the interior of Thrace but as the robbery of his possessions continued, he finally sailed back to Persia, to the satrap Pharnabazus. Bewitched by Alcibiades, now forty, who had lost none of his charm and little of his beauty, and who had known kings, princes, and generals, Pharnabazus offered him not only shelter but also the revenues from the town of Grynium. Believing he could do better, Alcibiades decided to see the great king himself, Artaxerxes II at Susa. He also knew of Lysander's contacts with Cyrus the Younger, and the attempts of both men to replace Artaxerxes with Cyrus. He felt he could advise Artaxerxes in how to avoid being overthrown by his younger brother, and how to avoid mounting problems with Sparta. Perhaps fearing that Alcibiades would enthrall Artaxerxes as he did Pharnabazus himself, Pharnabazus refused to help Alcibiades in his quest to travel to Susa. The Athenian left anyway. Lysander learned of his departure and informed Pharnabazus that if Alcibiades were not handed over alive or dead, Sparta would end all collaboration with Persia. Lysander, in turn, was being pressured by the oligarchy he had set up in Athens, men whose survival depended, they felt, on eliminating Alcibiades as a future menace to their very survival.

Alcibiades put in at a town along the way to Susa and, wanting company for the night, Cornelius Nepos tells us, took a young Arcadian, a loyal friend, to bed. Pharnabazus' men had followed him and very silently heaped brush around the habitation, which they then set on fire. Awoken by the light and crackling of the blaze, and guessing at its origin, Alcibiades flung his Spartan-style cloak around his left arm and took up his sword in his right hand. He and his friend threw as much clothing as possible on the blaze, making a narrow passage threw the flames. They leaped through a window and, naked, confronted men who immediately backed away. But they were outnumbered, and even from a distance many of their enemies' numerous spears and arrows hit their marks. Dead, Alcibiades was decapitated and his head bagged for Pharnabazus. His companion for a night, younger and faster, managed to escape.

But Plutarch maintains that Alcibiades had been killed by the brothers of a girl whom Alcibiades had seduced, and so his death had nothing to do with either Lysander or Pharnabazus. Both Nepos and Plutarch agree on what followed: Another friend, a whore, Timandra, found the headless body that she wrapped in his Spartan cloak and had cast into the blaze, a pyre worthy of that built for Achilles, Patroclus and Hector.

Exactly like the Sparta he loved and admired, Alcibiades is one of the strangest, most original, most enigmatic creatures to have adorned the Earth. Lustful, intelligent and beautiful, even in boyhood his admirers had made him aware of every erogenous zone on his body, far in advance of the friends his age. He knew human nature and weaknesses thanks to his enlightened guardian Pericles, whose home and bed were replenished by his whore mistress, Aspasia, and whose salon was graced by the greatest philosophers and dramaturges the world has known. Just as importantly he allowed his body to serve, valiantly in battle, erotically in sex. Charm, class, a come-hither regard that could stagger, an orator capable of enthralling an assembly, a manliness that inspired other men, a self-confidence that won over diamond-in-the-rough Spartans and cynically jaded Orientals. People were truly fond of him, they genuinely liked to be around him, and so exquisite did he know himself to be that when Socrates chose *not* to lie with him, he honestly admired the philosopher's unfathomable restraint before such perfection. In the whole world I can only think of Lorenzo *Il Magnifico* who comes close, if one can make abstraction of beauty and military expertise.

CHAPTER EIGHT

SOCRATES

The first of the great philosophers was Socrates. Cicero, who seems to have invited himself into any and all intellectual pursuits, says that Socrates was the first philosopher because it was he who brought philosophy down from the heavens and placed it in the agora and in the minds of men. Socrates said that no man wanted to commit evil and if he did, he did so through ignorance; virtue, therefore, was knowledge. Plato defined virtue as possessing four parts: temperance, prudence, courage and justice. Plato goes on to say that Socrates' role in Athenian society was to sting it into action. Socrates himself was recorded to have said that he was the gods' gift to Athens, a form of hubris that the Athenians hated. Alcibiades was known to have been Socrates' favored student and as he had blasphemed the gods through the destruction of the Hermes' statues, and as he had fled to Sparta thereby aiding Athens' mortal enemy, the partial blame fell on Socrates' shoulders, for which the philosopher was accused of corrupting the youth. Other of Socrates' students, as I've mentioned, had also taken shelter in Sparta. Socrates failed to believe in the rule of the masses, preferring a society governed by knowledgeable people and professional competence— an intellectual oligarchy. The historical context was also against Socrates. Athens had just been annihilated by Sparta as an empire and the Spartans had imposed a tyranny on the city, enforced by a body called the Thirty Tyrants. At its head was a certain Critias, a former student of Socrates. Now free again, Athenians wanted to punish any remnant of their former tragedy. A jury drawn by lot was chosen to judge Socrates, a simple majority carrying the decision. Plato came forward with an offer to pay any fine the assembly imposed on the philosopher but the assembly preferre death. He was then encouraged to flee but chose to drink hemlock instead. He was 70.

A few years before his death he was heard repeating the words of the poet Theognis:

> Damn youth; damn miserable age!
> The last for coming, the first for leaving.

Socrates, despite his ugliness, could hypnotize a boy with his rhetoric as easily as a cobra by the swaying of a flute. His power over Alcibiades was such that his words overwhelmed the boy, reducing him to tears. Plutarch tells us that Socrates was the only person capable of reaching the good side of the boy and stirring his heart. But then Alcibiades would abandon the philosopher, continues Plutarch, for the ''pleasures offered him by his flatterers.'' Then Socrates would pursue him as if ''he were a fugitive slave.''

In Plato's *Symposium* Alcibiades enters drunk, wearing a crown of ivy with flowers. He immediately drains a wine glass and in a stupor declares that his attraction to Socrates is the philosopher's resemblance to a satyr, an animal of gross appetites and monumental erections. He claims that he is a victim, as are all boys, to Socrates' rhetorical skills, stating that when Socrates speaks ''my heart beats wildly and tears stream down my face.'' For his part, Socrates claimed that the boy flew into fits of jealousy when he (Socrates) was with another lad, ''He yells at me and slaps me around,'' giving the impression, it seems to me, that they're in a gay bar during our own times. Socrates observed that Alcibiades' lovers only love his body, and that when he loses his bloom they will disappear, while he, Socrates, ''will always be there for him.'' Alcibiades prided himself on doing the outrages, so perhaps he really did convince himself that he was drawn to this ugly old brilliant man. That Socrates could continue to deny that he ever had the slightest intention of laying a lustful hand on the boy may or may not be true. The importance is that the two knew each other and were, if we believe Plato, direly influenced by their interaction. Thanks in part to Plato and Socrates, Alcibiades, in all his contradictions, has come down to us through the ages.

With age men like Plato and Socrates and scores of others had more and more difficulty seducing youths, as noted by Theognis:

> Your wondrous beauty you can offer me,
> And since I love you, it's no disgrace for me
> To beg. I pray you, on my hands and knees,
> Honor me, handsome boy, do what I ask;
> For some day you will face another boy.
> May you receive the same response you give me!

For just reason is Theognis known as the greatest homoerotic poet of antiquity.

Alcibiades knew that Socrates could give him everything he needed to complete his rise to political power: knowledge, argumentation, rhetoric, dialectic, strategizing and worldliness. As for Alcibiades, he had only his physical perfection to offer in return. He thusly invited the philosopher to a dinner in which he deployed his every charm. His surprise was great when his guest, finding that Alcibiades had dismissed all his servants, did not immediately make clear, in one of multiply forms that men employ to assuage their lust, his interest in the boy. In fact, after eating, Socrates rose to leave. Telling Socrates that the hour was late, Alcibiades suggested he remain the night. When he did so, Alcibiades crept into his bed, beside him, and told Socrates that he knew of no man as deserving as he to gain access to his beauty, and it would be stupid if they didn't seek pleasure one with the other. ''After all,'' continued the boy, ''who better than you can make of me a better person?'' Socrates agreed that it was indeed his aim to make him better, and so saying, he closed his eyes and man and boy spent the night … platonically. The next morning Alcibiades recounts that it was as if he had slept with his father or brother, and then goes on to add, with all the modesty of those who are beautiful, that he was forced to admire the inner strength of Socrates, because he had resisted the body of the lad a full night! And Theognis would agree that a lad in full bloom is a heck of a temptation! Xenophon confirms that Alcibiades needed Socrates because of the philosopher's immense ''competence in discourses and in strategic action.'' He adds that Alcibiades may have known about Socrates' total control over his impulses and was therefore certain to be able to offer himself without the slightest risk of being abused.

As the banquet proceeded, Socrates and Plato felt they had to absolve man-to-man/boy relationships by finding a virtuous justification for them. This was apparently easy in man-to-woman attachments because the man and the woman worked in a virtuous tandem, in that he gave his sperm and she became physically pregnant with a child, this being the first virtue; the second virtue resided in the fact that, thanks to his progeny, a man became immortal. Man-to-man/boy relations could be virtuous when the players passed on to each other knowledge and wisdom (especially when the lover did so to his beloved). The beloved became pregnant in terms of his soul, and his child was the virtue his lover had implanted in him (knowledge/wisdom). Socrates claimed that without this kind of insemination the sex act was useless. Because Alcibiades was incapable of giving virtue, said Socrates, he was doomed to mortality. For Alcibiades things were far simpler: the eroticism of his inseminating a handsome yout' was perfect fulfillment in itself. We don't know if these two philosophe

Socrates and Plato, succeeded in making the boy feel guilty, we don't know if they were even sincere in disseminating such nonsense. We do know that Alcibiades tried to seduce Socrates despite his age and ugliness, perhaps to show the philosopher that the philosopher really did care for the physical aspect of love, just like everyone else. (If Alcibiades were as handsome as the ancients say—and only half as wonderful as he thought himself to be—then the temptation must have been truly difficult for Socrates.) But we know for certain that when Alcibiades left the banquet he took a good breath of fresh air, and went straight to find a warm bed with a warm boy to fill it.

At any rate Alcibiades knew the truth of Theognis' words:

> I play, enjoying my youth. For I shall lie
> A long time under the earth, when life is gone.
> Deaf as a stone I'll leave forever the sun's warmth;
> Fine though I was, I shall see nothing more.

Whether in truth Socrates did manage to rein in his libido will never be known, but on this very scene from Plato's *Banquet* Cicero muses that it's nonetheless curious that men like Socrates and Plato, claiming to be sexually disinterested, are always willing to give a helping hand to beautiful boys like Alcibiades, but never ever to ugly ones.

Mimnermus of Ionian Smyrna stakes everything on beauty too, because once it's lost: ''Though previously most beautiful of men, when his season is gone, boys neither rate him nor love him, not even his sons love him.'' (The cruelty is mind-boggling.)

As in Rome, slaves could be used for sex but were forbidden from having sexual congress with a free boy (bizarrely, the law stipulated *boy* and said nothing about girls, who were perhaps too protected by their families to be in danger). Boy slaves were often put in male brothels. Socrates was said to have bought one, but whether for his personal use or to free him from prostitution is unknown. Anal sex with a foreigner was acceptable but looked on as demeaning. He who said that everything and anything is possible in sexuality hit the nail on the head. Boys were desirable to men only between puberty and the first whiskers on their chins and hair on their backsides, but often boys prolonged their staying power by simply carefully shaving both chins and cheeks. Men normally preferred to penetrate, but there were many other full-grown men who craved being scratched in the orifice where only an engorged penis could appease the itching. Theocritus delivers a scene which illustrates the degrading effect of intercourse when socially established rules, practiced by the noble were not followed. Here we have two shepherds:

Comatus: You remember when I stuck it to you and you grinned and moved your tail to and fro very nicely and held on to that oak tree?

Lacon: No, but I remember very well the time when Eumaras tied you up and gave you a fucking.

Amusingly, at the entrance to gardens and orchards were representations of Priapus whose massive erect member represented the threat that trespassers would be anally violated should they enter--the ultimate humiliation.

A huge difference between the Greeks and the Romans (if historians, after two thousand years, are correct) was that the Greeks preferred their boys with modest members, the perfect size to fit the anus and the mouth, whereas the Romans followed the cult of Priapus, and, as today, thought that bigger was always better. Clapping could be heard in the Roman baths when a man of healthy dimensions paraded through the corridors. One Roman, Cotta, was known to invite only guests to his lavish dinners whom he had first seen at the baths—a word often on his lips was donkey. On Greek plates satyrs always display a huge penis, while boys called handsome (*kalos*) invariably have small to very small members, the size which seems to have been the most admired. All Greek cocks also have long and very pointed forskins, even when they are fully erect. (On a personal note, it's indeed sad that today we mutilate your boys by circumcision, a decision that should be left to them when they're old enough to decide for themselves.)

In his *Symposium* Plato describes Socrates' visit to a gymnasium. The beautiful Critias comes to him, having heard that Socrates knows how to cure headaches. He sits down beside the philosopher and tells him that he is in pain. Socrates turned to examine him when the boy's cloak opens and ''I saw inside. I was on fire, absolutely beside my self.'' It was obvious that Socrates had glimpsed the boy's lower torso and genitals. It's a truism that no matter how often a man sees a boy naked, in the palaestra, the gymnasium, the wresting school, the locker room, on the Internet, it's never enough. In another scene Socrates tells Plato that there are two boys he would like to meet. Plato suggests they invite them to one of their discussions. It was obvious, here too, that this was one of their ways of procuring youths.

In Athens, one was as hypocritical as elsewhere. A father would protect the hymen of his daughter at all costs, but would be proud if his son took that of the neighbor girl. Dover tells us of a father of a fourteen-year-old lad who made the boy come straight home from the palaestra and ordered him to never ever talk to strange men. He was nevertheless pleased when rumor had it that his son had been caught screwing the fourteen-year-old neighbor boy (screwing but *not* being screwed, which made all the difference). Fathers much preferred that their sons sought pleasure with other boys because of the financial and social problems involved if he did so with a girl, getting her pregnant.

Socrates, who outlived Alcibiades, taught Alcibiades' son. The boy was so beautiful that Socrates warned those around him to beware: "The beast they call young and handsome is more dangerous than a scorpion. You needn't touch a boy as you do a scorpion to be poisoned. A boy, with just a look, can make you mad from a distance. So when you see a beautiful boy run for your life, take a year's holiday elsewhere as it will take that long to heal you."

Despite his ugliness but thanks to his intelligence, Socrates was Alcibiades' best friend. He had saved Alcibiades' life during the Battle of Delium, one of the minor Peloponnesian wars, a few years before. Socrates should have received a prize for valor, as was the custom, but the prize went instead to Alcibiades, due to his affluence, position and beauty, beauty that touched the generals who gave out the awards. Socrates demonstrated his love by seconding the generals' decision. During Plato's *Banquet* Alcibiades reminds Socrates that he had done all in his power to get the generals to change their minds, a declaration that both Plato and Socrates preferred not to comment. Like Alcibiades, Socrates was fearless, although unlike the boy, he was an accomplished strategist. He was an unequalled dialectician who would use the art of rhetoric--maintains a much later chronicler--to seduce many a lad, bewitching them with his golden tongue and, spreading his woolen cloak, the chlamys, in an isolated field, would take the pleasure offered by the lad's hairless thighs. Socrates had shared Alcibiades' tent at Delium and was known to be his lover, albeit no one seems to have gotten close enough to verify the fact. At any rate, Socrates had always claimed that his role was to protect the boy from his admirers who wished "to caress him", and in so doing protect the plant from "perishing in the flower." Socrates knew that Alcibiades' philosophy of life was that resumed by Theognis:

> Let's give our hearts to banquets, while we
> Can still find bliss in wondrous things.
> For glorious youth goes by as fast as lightening,
> Faster than horses charging recklessly,
> Bringing their masters to the fields of war,
> While they delight in the sweet wheat-bearing plain.

As mentioned, it was in part due to Socrates' influence on the highly unstable Alcibiades that led to Socrates being accused of corrupting the youth of Athens, which in turn led to his death. Corruption here didn't mean sexual corruption. Many of the boys Socrates had taught betrayed

Athens in one form or another, and so Socrates, in the back of peoples' minds, was responsible for having socratized them: The first person to dishonor the city was Alcibiades himself, who would soon to be banished and would take shelter with the Spartans; the second was the great historian Xenophon, his pupil, who would likewise be exiled to Sparta where he was given an estate; and, finally, his disciple Critias would one day be a member of an oligarchy called the Thirty, under Spartan influence, and be responsible for the deaths of many Athenian democrats. Even his follower Plato proposed an ideal state based on Sparta. In other words, Socrates would soon be condemned for being a Spartan fellow traveler.

We do have one concrete example of Socrates being less virginal than he would like one to believe. Once, visiting a shipyard in the company of Pericles, the philosopher nodded towards the carnal beauty of one of the sailors, bringing forth a reaction from Pericles, noted by Plutarch: ''A man should not only have clean hands but a clean mind as well.'' Pericles was noted for frequenting prostitutes and, alas, one of his sons, also called Pericles, was publicly taunted, Eupolis informs us, as being ''a whore's son.''

What I find particularly interesting about Plato and Socrates is their discussions on father-son relationships (as Socrates wrote nothing, these ''discussions'' come exclusively from Plato himself). Plato wonders to what extent a father's interest in his boys influences how they turn out. He wonders to what extent a boy's character is formed by his dad and the influence exerted on a boy by his brothers. (And why not his guardian? In which case it's difficult to see Pericles' influence on Alcibiades, except as a source of money, political contacts and reflected prestige.) Socrates is described as being a fatalist who mocked those like Pericles who shelled out funds to provide Alcibiades with the best tutors and trainers. Character, according to Socrates, is a gift of the gods, stemming perhaps from the fact that he himself had no father but turned out all right (his mother had been a midwife), thanks to the man-boy relationships he had known. He hinted that he was not close to his own sons, but so close to his pupils that they would sorely miss him when he was gone, stating that the boys would be ''fatherless'' without him. He also was aware of the passing of time, as in Theognis' words:

Those men are stupid fools who mourn the dead
And do not mourn the flower of lost youth.

Or if I may state it in my way, *Why does one mourn death--which is but eternal sleep--and not the coming of age, the veritable human night?*

CHAPTER NINE

THE SACRED BAND

The Sacred Band destroyed the Spartan army in 371 B.C., the first army to ever do so. The Spartans had been victorious against the Persians and had brought Athens to its knees during the Peloponnesian Wars. And now a group of Thebans destroyed its power forever. The cause of the war between the Spartans and Thebans was Spartan domination over a people that wanted its freedom, a people who had had enough of Spartans ever trying to force them into forming an oligarchy. The Thebans elected a general, Epaminondas, to confront them at the town of Leuctra. The outcome swung back and forth until Epaminondas gave the signal for his lover, Pelopidas, to enter the fray at the head of the Sacred Band of Thebes, lovers and their beloveds, who would unhesitatingly fight to the death rather than show themselves cowards in front of their comrades, and, especially, before he who had been chosen as a life companion. The Thebans allowed the Spartan survivors to leave with their dead, including their king, Cleombrotus, and then raised a trophy to their victory. But here the real victory was not over the Spartans, the veritable victory was the loyalty and friendship--the pledge of eternal love--begun years prior when Epaminondas had met the young, handsome and valiant Pelopidas, a truly unique figure in Greek history. Born rich and giving his life to attain the summits in athletics, Pelopidas squandered the family fortune on Theban poor. Plutarch tells us that when criticized for dilapidating his fortune, reminding him that money was a basic necessity, Pelopidas pointed to a blind and crippled pauper and said, ''Yes, it's necessary for him.'' He himself ate the simplest of foods and wore the plainest clothes. He rejoiced in the hardships of physical and militaristic training which took place in an atmosphere of soldierly friendships.

Epaminondas not only won at Leuctra, he and Pelopidas then entered the Peloponnese where they set free the Messenian helots, after generations of slavery. Naturally, Messenia became Thebes' most loyal and most grateful supporter.

The idea for the Sacred Band had been Pelopidas'. He modeled it after his friendship with Epaminondas, 150 lovers and 150 beloveds, men and boys who would never shy away from death if it meant betraying his lover's or his beloved's faith in him. Polyaenus describes the Sacred Band as being composed of men "devoted to each other by mutual obligations of love" and Plato describes a lover as being ''a friend inspired by god.'' The Theban general Pammenes had criticized Nestor of Trojan War fame when he organized his troops by tribe and clan and not by lovers and beloveds because, says Plutarch, ''Friendship grounded in love is never to be broken and is invincible, since lovers and beloveds, to avoid shame, will rush into danger to rescue one another.'' The perfect example was given during the Battle of Leuctra when one of the Sacred Band, ambushed, asked his enemy to run him through at the breast so that his lover would not blush at seeing a wound to the back. The Sacred Band never ever sought death for itself. To the contrary, they entered battle protected with armor and armed with the finest weapons. They spent their days in the palaestra training and learning strategy, but also in philosophy and singing and dancing. There was much discussion on tactics, a science Epaminondas was already famous for. Their bodies were sleek, oiled and kept clean by their companion who scraped the oil from the toned muscles with a strigil. They sweated in huts warmed by fired stones over which they splashed water. Plato tells us that ''love between males was so special in Thebes that is was illegal for anyone to maintain that sex between men was not beautiful.'' The Sacred Band was stationed on the Acropolis. Their service started at around age twenty and ended around age thirty. Pelopidas turned them into shock troops whose main function was killing enemy leaders by any means possible, thereby crippling the enemy.

We know this about the Theban Pammenes, who had criticized Nestor as mentioned above. When Philip of Macedon was a boy he was sent to Thebes and placed under the care of the great general Pammenes, an ardent boy-lover, who immediately reserved the young and willing prince for his bed. Later, when Philip was king of Macedon, his general Pausanias came to him with the complaint that he had been forcefully sodomized. Pausanias felt that he had the king's ear because they too had been lovers when young. Pausanias claimed that he had had relations with a boy who killed himself when Pausanias threw him over for another. The boy's former lover, a certain Attalus, decided to wreck vengeance on Pausanias by inviting him to a banquet, during which he forcefully raped Pausanian after getting him drunk. Pausanias hoped that King Philip would avenge the outrage by killing Attalus. But Attalus was both an essential general in Philip's army and the father of Philip's wife. So to placate Pausanias, Philip named him to his personal guard, affording Pausanias the proximity he needed to drive a dagger into Philip's chest—thus opening the way for Philip's son, the Great Alexander. Pausanias, in turn, was cut down by Philip's guard. History can be crueler still: The Sacred Band liberated Thebes from Spartan domination and won its freedom until it was totally destroyed by Alexander, he who was said to have known defeat only once in his life, when confronting the thighs of his lover Hephaestion.

Cicero called Epaminondas ''the first man of Greece.'' Centuries later Montaigne named Epaminondas as being one of three of the world's ''worthiest men,'' the other two being Homer and Alexander the Great. We know of Epaminondas and Alexander's preferences, but nowhere in Homer's writings does he mention male-male relations. Most aspects of Epaminondas' reputation have been lost in the mists of time due to the fact that just a score of years after his passing Alexander obliterated Thebes, thusly destroying his and Pelopidas' heritage. He is also less known because we have, thanks to Plutarch, the life of Pelopidas, while that of Epaminondas was lost. But we do have traces of his past due to Cornelius Nepos and Diodorus Siculus. As a boy he favored wrestling, running and prowess in the handling of weapons. What the poets call the defining moment of his life occurred during the Battle of Mantinea, in 385 B.C., an earlier battle when Thebes fought on the side of Sparta. Here he saved Pelopidas' life. Epaminondas had noticed the boy in camp, and when he came upon him during the fighting, slumped on the ground amid the bodies of his comrades, apparently dead, as his body had been rended in six places by sword and spear thrusts. Epaminondas now stood his ground above him, he too receiving wounds to the chest by a spear and on the arm by a sword. He in turn was saved by the Spartan king Agesipolis who arrived in the nick of time with his men. Times change as do alliances and Thebes found itself fighting innumerable skirmishes against the Spartans until the city-state was forced to bend to Spartan will. The Spartans occupied the Acropolis and set up a puppet regime but, incredibly, allowed Epaminondas to remain because he was poor and the Spartans equated his poverty with impotence. Other Thebans had been forced to leave, among them Pelopidas. Both men, one inside and one outside, now prepared those around them for a revolt against the Spartans. When ready, Pelopidas led his men into the city where, with the aid of his lover, they killed the city's governing body in their beds. They then set siege to the Acropolis. The Spartans, in a rare move for them, agreed to surrender if they could leave with their lives. This was granted and Thebes was again free. The victory was especially important because, for the first time, Sparta was seen as being assailable.

Epaminondas and Pelopidas then went to the shrine of Iolaus where they offered up thanks. Iolaus had been another member of the Argonauts and another of Heracles' lovers. Heracles--sexually insatiable--had been a follower of the poet who wrote that ''True pleasure in sex came only through changing partners.'' He believed so to the extent that he offered the boy, then age sixteen, to his wife, age thirty, with whom the boy had a child. The gymnasium in Thebes was called the Iolaus and athletic games to the boy were known as the Iolaeia. Plutarch states that men and their beloveds exchanged sacred vows of love at the shrine of Iolaus. And according to Aristotle, same-sex couples ''invoked his name to guarantee their oaths of faith and to punish faithless lovers.''

It's amusing to note that during the games--Nemean, Panathenaea or Olympic--"boys never touched women or other boys in the whole period when they are at the peak of their training." Just like today.

Epaminondas and Pelopidas virtually governed Thebes together, Pelopidas, with the fire of youth, was recognized as the most aggressive of the two in his support of measures that systematically reduced Spartan strength throughout the region. Then followed the Battle of Leuctra as described above, after which came the liberation of the helots. Then, incredibly, Epaminondas was put on trial back in Thebes for a crime punishable by death. To understand what went on, one has to known that Greeks held to certain principles, principles that were of vital importance to them, but at times made them lose the overall perspective of things, an example of not being able to see the forest for the trees. Epaminondas' crime was that during his expedition to Sparta to free the helots he had remained in power a little longer than the time when his term in office expired. So at his trial Epaminondas read out a prepared statement. He told the Thebans that after putting him to death they were to raise a stele in his honor on which it would be inscribed that here lies Epaminondas who saved the Thebans from Spartan tyranny at the Battle of Leuctra and then went on to chase them back to the Peloponnesus, thusly saving all of Greece from their tyranny, before invading said Peloponnesus in order to liberate their slaves, the helots.

Luckily for Epaminondas, the Thebans had more of a sense of humor than did the Athenians. They broke out in laughter and freed their savior. Of course, all of this is highly abridged. In truth, what happened to Epaminondas throughout all his life is what happened to every important man throughout all of Greece, from Themistocles to Pericles, as well as to even the great philosophers like Socrates: Greeks have always been jealous of other Greeks and have always tried to trip them so they would land face down in the mud. This happened time and time again to Epaminondas and Pelopidas but I won't get into the silly details. The essential is that both men always came out on top, politically speaking.

As proof of this, Athens, grown weary of Thebe's new power and eternally angry because Thebes had taken the side of the enemy during the Persian Wars, joined Sparta and the Mantineians in a final battle against Thebes, the outcome of which would so weaken Athens, Sparta and even Thebes that Philippe of Macedon's ambition of conquest would be greatly facilitated. It will be remembered that during the first Battle of Mantinea, in 385 B.C., Epaminondas and Pelopidas fought on the Spartan side. It was during this battle that Epaminondas saved Pelopidas' life and they became fast friends and lovers. This, again, was the first battle of Mantinea.

Two years before the second Battle of Mantinea Pelopidas was sent to Pherae to end the aggressive ambitions of a local dictator, Alexander of

Pherae. He was at the head of a group of mercenaries who abandoned him when they took fear due to an eclipse of the sun. Pelopidas went on anyway with a much-reduced force. He won the battle but Alexander escaped. It was during his pursuit that Pelopidas, riding ahead of his men, was waylaid and murdered. Alexander himself, Plutarch informs us, was later assassinated by his wife, tired of his tyranny towards her: Alexander slept in a chamber at the top of a tower, the door of which was guarded by a ferocious chained dog. His wife lured the dog away and covered the steps leading to Alexander's bedroom with wool so he would not hear her three brothers approach. His body was pierced with a hundred stab wounds and thrown from the tower to the street below where it was torn to shreds by his compatriots, who also had had enough of him.

During the second Battle of Mantinea, Sparta had become the enemy. Little by little what should have been a limited engagement turned into the biggest battle in the history of Greece, with a cast of thousands. Epaminondas had his troops march parallel with those of his enemy, but in a leisurely fashion, as if they didn't intend to fight that day. Some of his troops even stopped to bivouac. When he felt the enemy had sufficiently relaxed its guard, he ordered an all-out attack. Diodorus tells us that the Athenians and Spartans were undone by the rain of missiles hurled by the Sacred Band, after which, says Xenophon, Epaminondas "forced his army through the ranks of the enemy like the prow of a trireme." The Sacred Band came at the Spartans with reserve forces that broke their phalanx, forcing them to flee. The battle would have ended in a route if Epaminondas had not been fatally struck in the chest by a spear thrown from the Mantineian ranks. The spear broke, leaving the iron point deep in the heart. The Thebans immediately ended their pursuit, a testament to Epaminondas' eminence. Both sides returned their dead, and both sides put up trophies as if both had won. As was customary, Epaminondas was buried on the battlefield. He was renown as an incorruptible man of ascetic tastes and, as he said during his trial, he had humbled Sparta and freed Messenia. Internecine warfare would continue among Greeks, but this was in their nature: As Shakespeare aptly wrote, "The fault, Brutus, is not in the stars but in ourselves." Epaminondas' life had been dedicated to his country and his lover, he had never married, never fathered a son to avenge his death, as Aegisthus avenged his father Thyestes, as Orestes avenged Agamemnon, as was written on the Mycenaean stele: *Son My, Avenger My.*

Epaminondas and Pelopidas were far from the only same-sex couples in Thebes. Philolaus gave laws to the Thebans and he and his lover, the famous Diocles, an Olympic runner and victor, lived together until their deaths. Diocles had been forced to leave his native home, Corinth, due to the incestuous passion of his mother. Male friends visited their tombs which were side by side but pointed in different directions: Philolaus' was pointed towards Thebes and Diocles' towards Corinth.

An epigram on a tombstone, concerning the Sacred Band, has been recently found with this inscription: "Direct your arrows, dear Eros, at these bachelors, that, bold in the love they share they will defend their fatherland, for your arrows fire boldness and of all the gods you, Eros, are supreme at exalting front-line champions."

CHAPTER TEN

ARISTOTLE-ALEXANDER-HEPHAESTION

In this chapter I've decided to touch on the sexual relationship between Alexander the Great and Hephaestion while recounting that of Aristotle, their teacher. Aristotle was born in the town of Stagira, to the far north of Greece, in a kind of three-tentacled peninsula called Chalcidice. His father was a physician which should have been Aristotle's career too, as being a physician in Greece at the time was a heritage handed down from father to son. But he died when Aristotle was ten, the same age that Alcibiades lost his father, and like Alcibiades, Aristotle was of the nobility and well-off financially.

At the time the region was under the thumb of the Macedonian king Amyntas III. Very exceptionally Amyntas lived to the ripe old age of 80, an exception in a country nearly as savage as Thrace, where sons, uncles, nephews and brothers killed each other off with what seemed to be innate talent. I won't go into all the vendettas, so suffice it to say that three of Amyntas' sons eventually became king: Alexander II, Perdiccas II and Philip II, father of the Great Alexander (III). Philip III reigned an impressive 23 years. The line of Amyntas III would end with Alexander the Great.

We know that Aristotle had at least one brother, unnamed, who produced a son that fought with Alexander but, when he refused to prostrate himself before Alexander in the Persian manner, Alexander had him tortured under the suspicion of fomenting a revolt and put to death.

At age 17 Aristotle went to Athens, the big city of 150,000, as one goes, today, to New York. Other city-states in Greece had populations that rarely exceeded 40,000. As war was an Athenian constant, Aristotle estimated that 2,000 Athenians a year died in battle.

There were two schools at the time of Aristotle's' arrival, that of Isocrates and that of Plato. Isocrates' school was based on rhetoric, training for public speakers and lawyers, a sure guarantee of wealth. Speakers In Athens were highly praised and often elected to important positions. Every educated Greek was expected to speak convincingly, whatever the subject, and could win prizes of considerable value. Isocrates was rich thanks to his father who manufactured flutes and, like his father, he had a good head for business, charging his pupils 1,000 drachmae, a huge sum. Plato's school was more liberal, and it was there that Aristotle chose to go, perhaps in part because Plato accepted Macedonians more readily, a people that most Athenians found course and dominating. Courses were free for those who couldn't pay. Plato had been an accomplished athlete in his youth, trained in gymnastics. He gave up an athletic career when he heard Socrates speak. Plato is known to have loved a certain Aster, meaning ''star''. He wrote, ''You gaze at the stars, my Star; were I Heaven so that I could gaze at you with many eyes.'' He also loved Agathon, described as the handsomest boy in Athens: ''When I kiss Agathon my soul is on my lips.'' Plato's classes took place in the Academy, land left to him by a man named Academus. It contained statues and sepulchers, plane trees and olive groves, and, eventually, Plato's tomb. The school would go on for 900 years.

Dion, 21, was a student of particular interest to Plato. He wrote this to the handsome lad: ''O Dion who makes my heart mad with love for you.'' Dion came from Syracuse and convinced Plato to return home with him in order to establish his ideal republic by teaching its present dictator, Dionysius. When Dionysius proved to be immune to education in any form, Plato told him he was a fool and a tyrant. Dionysius retaliated by selling Plato into slavery! Luckily a friend bought and then freed him.

When Dionysius died, Dion asked him to return and tutor his heir and son, Dionysius II. Still mad about the boy, Plato agreed. Dionysius II proved teachable but highly influenced by his entourage that convinced him that Plato was going to turn Syracuse over to the Athenians, after having made Dion the new king. Dionysius reacted by banishing Dion to Italy and locking up Plato in his castle where he nevertheless continued on as Plato's student. A war broke out and Dionysius, perhaps fearing for Plato's life, freed him. When the war ended he wanted Plato back, but the philosopher naturally refused until Dionysius told him that in that case he would seize all of Dion's holdings in Syracuse, reducing the boy to poverty. However, if Plato agreed to come back, Dion would be given permission to return to Syracuse to be reunited with Plato. Still in love, Plato took the first ship. But things soured between Plato and Dionysius, and Dion was again expulsed and Plato banished. Dion raised an army and invaded Sicily at the side of another of Plato's students, the Athenian general Callippus. Dionysius fled and Dion was installed as king. From his exile Dionysius paid a succession of assassins to infiltrate Dion's friends and murder them, one by one. He then bribed Callippus with enough money to run Dion through with his sword. But instead of relinquishing the throne for Dionysius as was planned, Callippus took it for himself. He took Dion's wife Arete too, but when he became suspicious that she was plotting with Dionysius, he had her jailed, where she gave birth to Callippus' child. Dionysius finally raised an army large enough to win back his throne. Callippus retreated to Italy. If this were not enough, Callippus decided to win back the throne and recuperate his newly born son. He raised an army of mercenaries that he treated so badly that one of them killed him, supposedly with the sword Callippus had used on Dion.

Despite his obvious love for Dion, Plato was nonetheless a kind of Athenian Tartuffe. He often asserted that he was disinterested in boys physically, from whence we have our word platonic. At any rate, he got an evident kick out of putting Socrates in the erotic situations that he himself would have certainly enjoyed. An example is his accompanying Socrates to a wrestling school where the handsome Critias entered naked amidst a group of friends with whom he was arguing. Socrates "marveled at the boy's stature and beauty, and felt that everyone else in the room was in love with the boy," but Plato knew in advance that he would never have access to such perfection. Plato often used Aristophanes to express his own opinions, as when he was supposed to have written these words for the playwright to use in a play: "While they are boys they love men and like to lie with them and embrace them, and these are the best of the boys and youths. The evidence is that it's these boys, when they grow up, who become the best men in politics."

Plato believed in person-to-person dialogue which could, by its own dynamics, lead to insight into the minds of the persons exchanging views, the outcome being the discovery of truth. Aristotle spent years as an observer rather than a participant. As with karate, in the Academia one had to work one's way up from white belt to black belt 9th dan, which was eventually the case for Aristotle, although compared to Socrates (9th dan) he was perhaps 7th. Aristotle developed a system that allowed him to completely dissect a subject, to see it from every possible angle, the end being, as stated above, the discovery of truth. The Roman Cicero praised Aristotle's works as "rivers of gold." Alas, nearly nothing remains other than minute fragments.

In 343 B.C. Philip II invited Aristotle to his court to give instruction to Alexander, age 13, and his inseparable companion Hephaestion. Aristotle considered Hephaestion a far more assiduous student than Alexander and noted that Alexander shared all his secrets with the boy who was "by far his dearest friend." As they were the same age they most probably shared each other's bodies in equal measure, neither one being predominantly the lover or the beloved. Athenaeus says that Alexander "had a boundless passion for beautiful boys." He, Hephaestion and their friends certainly practiced sex from the very onset of puberty, an act as prevalent and shared as boys pissing in each other's presence. In addition to early circle-jerk-like inquisitiveness, they moved on, as did all Greek boys in the total absence of girls, to sex that was largely intercrural, one of the boys lying on his stomach or leaning against a wall while the other entered his closed thighs from behind, kissing his ears and neck and reaching around to give pleasure to his friend's manhood. All other forms of physical release were assuredly, at times, present. Their friendship was compared—by their friends—as resembling that between Achilles and Patroclus.

Philip turned over the shrine of the Nymphs at Mieza as a study room for the boys and their companions, and in thanks for Aristotle's services he rebuilt Aristotle's hometown of Stagira that he had previously destroyed when the town offered resistence to his army.

A moving story recounted by Aristotle concerns an uncontrollable horse that the boy Alexander managed to break in, the legendary Bucephalas. When he jumped down his father, an incredibly harsh man, went to him shedding tears, kissed him and told him to find a kingdom worthy of him, as Macedonia was far too small. Aristotle taught him the art of medicine as he himself had been instructed before his father's early death, instruction that continued afterwards thanks to other members of his family who wanted to see Aristotle follow in his father's steps. Alexander always carried a copy of Homer's *Iliad*, that he kept under his pillow with his dagger. Dionysius of Halicarnassus informs us that Alexander, Hephaestion and their companions were Aristotle's pupils for eight years. Because Plato had failed in reforming Dionysius II in Syracuse, it's possible that Aristotle hoped to succeed with Philip, especially as they were the same age. Aristotle may have lost prestige when, later, his nephew Callisthenes turned on Alexander and was executed. Plutarch seems to confirm this possibility, saying that when Aristotle arrived Alexander loved him as much as he did his own father, "for his father gave him life while Aristotle taught him how to live life." But then things changed and Alexander only remained with Aristotle because of his unquenchable thirst for knowledge. (One has the impression that Alexander's mind was incredibly mobile, flashing from one philosophy to another, shifting from tutor to tutor, idea to idea, as he did sexually from boy to boy, although Hephaestion was most assuredly the love of his life, especially as Hephaestion was always, irrevocably, his staunchest pillar.)

Alexander and Hephaestion formed a partnership during which Hephaestion commanded troops, built bridges, went on diplomatic missions, founded new settlements, as well as the incredible multitude of other tasks necessary when one rode with Alexander. During the siege of Tyre Alexander turned over the fleet to him, a difficult enterprise as the men he commanded had been conquered by Alexander's army and were thusly not the most responsive of allies.

When Hephaestion died from fever in Ecbatana at age 32, Alexander was prostrated with grief. He sent to the Oracle at Siwa to ask if he could deify his lover. The Oracle allowed him to make Hephaestion a divine hero, which seems to have satisfied him. At the time of his own death, a year later, Alexander was still making plans for the monuments, cities and shrines to be erected in his companion's honor.

Hephaestion had been sent to Athens to work out a reconciliation with Demosthenes, an orator of immense importance who had first opposed the military advances of Philip II, and then those of Alexander himself. Known for his love of boys, it's not impossible that this was a reason why Alexander dispatched the handsome Hephaestion. History's judgement of Demosthenes is unsavory. He had inherited great wealth and surrounded himself with youths, Aristion, Cnosion, Moschus, Aristarchus, to name a very few, whom he prostituted to augment his income. Demosthenes was thought to have been sexually passive, a highly disrespected role for a man in Athens where the act was reserved for boys, the penetrated always considered to be either a youth or someone unacceptably effeminate, which was most probably Demosthenes' case. To gain the favors of noble youths, Demosthenes did not hesitate to promise them ascendance over Athenians, thanks to the oratorical skills they would learn from him, an ancient casting couch. Once he gained control over a wealthy boy he would do what he could to despoil him.

Domosthenes was guilty of breaking two Athenian laws. The first stated that any Athenian who prostituted himself, and then made himself known in a public sense (speaking before the Assembly, for example) could be stoned to death. As Dover writes: ''If an Athenian citizen made no secret of his prostitution, did not present himself for the allocation of offices by lot, declared his unfitness if through someone's inadvertence he was elected to office, and abstained from embarking on any of the procedures forbidden to him by the law, he was safe from prosecution and punishment.'' The second law had a similar penalty for those who showed hubris. As Dover says, ''Hubris is a term applied to any kind of behavior in which one treats other people just as one pleases, with an arrogant confidence that one will escape paying any penalty for violating their rights and disobeying any law or moral rule accepted by society.'' Both Domosthenes and Alcibiades were multiple offenders of hubris. But, again, both were protected in high places.

There was, however, an ''amusing'' quirk in the law against hubris. If a man did what he pleased with a woman, if he arrogantly used her, *raped* her, this was clearly hubris according to the Athenians. But he couldn't be accused of hubris if he did so because of uncontrollable, *unpremeditated*, sexual lust, then this was no longer hubris and he could get off scot-free (although he could, naturally, be brought to trial for having broken other laws forbidding rape than those concerning hubris).

Surviving Greek amphorae, plates, bowls and twin-handled cups show boys playing sexual games and adult men fucking other adult men, but the practice was little spoken of as the passive partner was often, like Demosthenes, a subject of ridicule.

When Philip was assassinated, Demosthenes offered up public thanks to the gods and tried to convince Athenians to fight on the side of the countries who revolted when the death became known. But when the Athenians saw with what incredible rapidity and savagery his son took things in hand, they sent a delegation to plead for his forgiveness, a plea that Alexander acquiesced to.

Shortly afterwards a boyhood friend of Alexander, Harpalus, asked for sanctuary in Athens after stealing a great deal of money. In fact, this was the third time he had fled from Macedonia with funds that were not his own, but as Harpalus had been a close companion, Alexander had always forgiven him. The Athenians granted him asylum and the money he came to Athens with was put in Demosthenes' care. Of the 700 talents, a fabulous sum, 350 disappeared. While an enquiry went on Harpalus fled to Crete and Demosthenes fled to Aegina. Demosthenes was found guilty but the Athenians felt he was of such importance that a ship was sent to bring him home.

It was at this moment that Hephaestion was sent to Athens to work out a settlement. Demosthenes' answer was to spread the rumor that Alexander, on campaign in Thrace, had been killed, as had his entire army. Hephaestion left for Thrace where he found his friend and his army intact. Furious, Alexander began to march towards Athens but an Athenian delegation caught up with him and, again, begged forgiveness. It was accorded but only if Demosthenes were turned over to him. Demosthenes preferred poison to being captured and executed by Alexander's men. Thusly ended the life of this unsavory personage, as later, in Rome, the equally detestable Caligula and Nero would meet their fates.

Hephaestion was no poof. Parmenion was one of Alexander's greatest generals, a man Alexander could always depend upon. His son, Philotas, was one of Alexander's most trusted companions but due to accusations we know little about, he was charged with fomenting a revolt against the king. Hephaestion insisted that he be tortured, and undertook the duty himself. Found guilty, he was executed. But before the news could reach his father, Alexander had Parmenion murdered too. Hephaestion was appointed, along with Cleitus, joint commanders of Alexander's personal guard, the Companion Cavalry. Hephaestion was in agreement with his lover that the Macedonians and Persians should integrate. Indeed, he was Alexander's torchbearer, his best man, when Alexander married Roxana. Cleitus, and the older guard, were against Alexander's adoption of Persian ways. It was because Aristotle's nephew refused to kowtow to Alexander that he was now killed.

Just a words on Roxana. She bore Alexander's son, the future Alexander IV, posthumously. When word came of Alexander's death she had his second wife, Stateira, and his third wife, Parysatis, assassinated. She then put herself under the protection of Alexander's mother, Olympias. Alexander's friends, all former students of Aristocles, united and nominated one of them, Cassander, to take Alexander's place in Macedonia, and act as regent for his son Alexander IV. Instead, he had Roxana and Alexander, age 13, poisoned, along with a bastard son of Alexander, Heracles, whose mother was the daughter of the Persian satrap Artabazus. With these three dead he turned his attention to Alexander's mother, Olympias, whom he brought to trial, after promising her her freedom should she put herself in his hands peacefully. Instead, she was condemned to death and Cassander turned her over to the relatives of those she had killed—and they were legion. Her body was torn to pieces and she was thrown into the wild without last rites or a tomb. Cassander died from the swelling of his members, dropsy, in bed.

Back to Alexander and Hephaestion.

They crossed into India together at the head of hundreds of elephants, together they descended the Indus to the sea. Aristotle had described the two lovers as "One soul in two bodies." This proved to be the case when they both came to Troy, home—thanks to Homer—of the most famous battle in the history of mankind. They laid a wreath on the tomb of Achilles and Patroclus and it was at that moment that Alexander declared that his friendship with Hephaestus was in every point identical to the love between Achilles and Patroclus. They then ran a race, naked, in honor of the two heroes. Claudius Aelianus, the Roman author and teacher, states that "Alexander laid a garland on Achilles' tomb, Hephaestion on Patroclus'," meaning that it was Alexander, the lover, and Hephaestion the beloved, signifying that Alexander inseminated Hephaestion--but most sources believe that Patroclus, older than Achilles, was the inseminator. Yet Alexander and Hephaestion were the same age, which certainly implies that they shared all the possibilities of love making without the slightest interest concerning what was customary and what wasn't. Alexander was Hephaestion's lover, friend, king and commander, but would this count in matters sexual? Plutarch tells us that in bed together, they would go through Alexander's correspondence. When there was a letter that Alexander wanted kept secret, he would touch his ring to his lover's lips, a wondrously moving example of gay love, spanning so many centuries, so incredibly numerous life spans, all thanks to Plutarch, certainly as stirred as the reader. And, lastly concerning their intimacy, we have the quote from Diogenes of Sinope who maintains that the only time Alexander was ever vanquished, was by the thighs of Hephaestion.

Another proof of love, some suggest, was Alexander's request that Hephaestion marry his second wife's sister and daughter of Darius. Up until then Hephaestion's name was never mentioned concerning either another man or a woman. Four months after Hephaestion's marriage he was dead, of fever, probably typhus, in Ecbatana. Alexander had been away and didn't arrive back in time to tell his friend goodbye. Plutarch says that his "grief was uncontrollable." Alexander had the tails and manes of all the horses shorn and banned music of any sort. One source states that he flung himself on the body and was only dragged away by force, another that "he lay stretched upon the corpse all day and the whole night."

In memory of Achilles and Patroclus he had the entire tribe of Cossaeans decimated. You may remember that "at the pyre, Achilles gave his eternal farewell to Patroclus. He did it simply, respecting even in death his lover's modesty. The corpse was lifted onto the platform. Below, into the gutters between the edge of the pit and the logs, the animals were sacrificed, the jars of food, oil and wine were emptied and the captured Trojans were condemned to die. Each of the twelve was on his knees facing the logs. Each had his hands roped behind his back. All waited their turn as Achilles himself passed behind, pushed his knee into their spines, pulled back their heads by the hair, and slit their throats with Patroclus' own dagger. Their lives, valiant manhood and beauty ebbed rapidly down their chests and formed puddles where they fell after being shoved into the pit." (1)

As mentioned, the Oracle at Siwa allowed Alexander to have the boy worshipped as a divine hero, but not as a god. Funeral games with 3,000 competitors took place. A pyre 180 feet high, with steps, was raised. It was decorated with ships and banners and figures of armed warriors, torches with snakes entwining them, golden wreaths and eagles, lions and bulls and arms taken from the enemy. Diodorus recounts that Alexander had the sacred flame in the temple extinguished, an honor exclusively reserved for the deaths of the great Persian kings themselves.

As for Alexander, he died a year later, at age 33, also of fever, also typhus. Some say Aristotle was present. His body was placed in a gold sarcophagus and filled with honey. On its way to Macedonia it was stolen by Ptolemy and taken to Memphis. His successor, Ptolemy II, transferred it to Alexandria where it was later replaced by one made of glass. There is lies today, under unknown sands.

As with Achilles and Patroclus, as with Harmodius and Aristogeiton, Alexander and Hestaestion represent the very best in a couple: loyalty, ambition, the quest for knowledge, the utter refusal of passivity. All six were united when they were young and beautiful, when their bodies could achieve the utmost in adventure and passion. They all died young too, a terrible sacrifice, indeed, but one that spared them the ravages of demeaning old age.

Back in Athens Aristotle opened his own school that was called the Lyceum, but also the Peripatetic, meaning ''to walk around'', due to his habit of strolling with his students while teaching them. (Amusingly, the name for a whore, in French, is *péripatéticenne* because they too walk around, although the common French word is *putain*.) According to antique historians Aristotle had love affairs with several of his adolescent students, among them the 'ravishing'' Nicanor. Because of something he said, he was accused of heresy by Athenians who were ridiculously thin-skinned on the subject. To avoid Socrates' fate he fled home to the Chalcidice where he died at age 62, extremely young when one considers that nearly all the philosophers at the time lived to their 80s or 90s, (a quirk that continues to this very day).

POSTSCRIPT

The Greeks were fortunate in having been able to choose in which direction they could assuage their lust. Most of us today are not that fortunate. Socrates could bring tears to the eyes of Alcibiades, which is like bringing tears to the eyes of a rent-boy--not the easiest of things to do. He could convince a boy to share his cloak on a field outside the palaestra. The boy was no worse for the wear because both he and Socrates shared the same sexuality. Not all did, it seems: My favorite story is about the boy who just didn't like other boys *in that way*. As he was different from his friends-- and he hated being different--he asked Zeus to help him love boys. When this didn't happened, he killed himself. Today we have bisexual boys who, like the Greeks, *can* pick and choose. But most people seem to be like me, determined by homosexuality or heterosexuality.

In my Introduction I wrote: ''The decision to write this book has its origin in a recent law in France, where I live, allowing gay marriage. Legally, I was suddenly worth any other guy in this wonderful land.'' The logical next step was to prove that I really am worth other guys, guys like Travas Pastrano of double-back-flip fame—meaning that gays in general merit the same stature as straights. Naturally, nearly since birth I've been aware of men who shared my sexual orientation, da Vinci, Michelangelo, Rimbaud, Wilde, Tchaikovsky et al, but what I needed was the stories of less ethereal, more down to earth guys. As I've been preparing a book on Greece for years, I thought that that would be an excellent place to begin: I'd choose and relate the lives of Greeks whose preferences were similar to mine (after which I'd go on to Rome for Volume Two and then to Florence, the three places I love the most in the world). How astonished was I to discover, when I started sifting through my personal Greek heroes, that they *all*, or nearly all, had a marked attraction for boys. Only concerning Pericles was I unable to find a source relating any known experience with youths, and although I'm personally certain he had them, nothing of a concrete nature has come to light, the reason why I refer to Pericles on numerous occasions in my book, but never in a man-to-man/boy context.

I'm grateful for the French gay-marriage law that gives me a little self respect after a boyhood of great turbulence, and who knows, one day there may even be a law, like in ancient Thebes, proclaiming "that it is illegal for anyone to maintain that sex between men is not beautiful." (*On peut toujours rêver !*)

As I've said, this book has been in preparation for years. At the end you'll find the **SOURCES** I've consulted, scores of ancient poets, historians, logographers, chroniclers, playwrights, orators and philosophers; scores of other books as background concerning Greek history in general, wars, politics, economics, government, clothing and other nonsexual material; and, naturally, books dedicated to the explanation of the workings of homoeroticism in Greece, but thanks to the ancient sources I've consulted—the writers alive at that time or around that time—these books served only as checks-and-balances to ensure that I've made the fewest possible errors.

This work is aimed at gays in the hopes that they will find solace in the myriads of wonderful men who preceded us, especially Greeks who, I hope I've convinced you, were veritable heroes. This work is also aimed at bisexuals who have the choice. Normally a bisexual today is around 70% gay. If he were 50/50 he would most probably choose nearly exclusively girls in order to avoid being called all the names for queers that he hears in the locker room, and that from earliest childhood. So just maybe some of these 50/50, thanks to my book, will also try their hand at boy-love. As for heterosexuals, this book is an attempt to show why they should stop calling guys like me all those locker-room adjectives, why we deserve a minimum of respect. I know I'll never be accepted on the quay here in Capbreton where I have my little sailboat, and I couldn't care less. These hicks have never even heard of the likes of Socrates and Alcibiades. But most heterosexuals are far from being hicks so maybe one or two will listen with an indulgent ear. Maybe even those who are 80 or 90% hetero will be tempted to do even more! Lastly, this is something I learned from Marlon Brando: If you're ever in doubt, just listen to your dick. It's the only part of your anatomy that doesn't lie. When it gets hard, go in the direction it's pointing.

Even in ancient Greece where men were sexually ambivalent the question of why one was attracted to boys and not girls, or vice versa, was posed. We know that fathers wanted their sons to be handsome so as to attract a lover who would educate him, offer him gifts and, ideally, a good place in society. But what of the homely boys, those who even the so-called virtuous Plato or Socrates turned their backs on? And how honest were these great philosophers and noblemen like Alcibiades who knew the art of seducing a lad too young to have experienced life? Some men seemed to have preferred women because their milky attractiveness lasted so much longer. Boys, on the other hand, soon grew beards on their once downy chins, their suntanned skin roughened, their thighs and asses became hairy, and their innocence turned rebellious thanks to the knowledge they acquired with maturity. The boy who is becoming a man no longer lets his lover take his pleasure—a joy beyond compare, as one poet puts it—and then leave him once his lust is fulfilled, abandoning the boy with sore buttocks and only his hand for release.

Then again, the life of a boy, compared to that of a girl, can be so simple: He rises in the morning not needing even to shave as his cheeks are hairless. Just a little water splashed on his face will do him, then he pulls his chiton down over his head to his knees and he is no longer naked. Off to the gymnasium with his scrolls or tablets to learn rhetoric and perhaps an hour on his lyre, followed by athletics to strengthen his body or horsemanship or the use of weapons. At the palaestra he oils himself and his friends and wrestle in the noonday heat. Then the fun of scraping off the oil, a bath, a rapid meal and back to his tutors and stories of ancient heroes and the virtues that made them heroic. Dinner and bed with his lover, he who offers protection and instruction, knowledge and pleasure. A woman's day begins with cosmetics and artifices and ornaments meant to trick men so easily tricked. But let's spy on the queen of queens, Hera herself, as she prepares for Zeus' bed, an extreme example, perhaps, but highly enlightening: In the inner courtyard of the palace she immersed herself in the warm, limpid waters of her private pool. Fifty nymphs cleansed her ivory-white limbs and rinsed her flowing ringlets with precious griffin milk from coral-colored conches, while around the banks other nymphs looked on from beside marble lions' heads that spouted azure cascades into the tepid basin. Heavenly Mother allowed herself to be escorted up the steps leading out of the pool where she was wrapped in Coan silk with freshly-sewn rose petals that took away the moisture and scented her ample form. She reclined on a high lounge of pink damask and allowed herself to be oiled and massaged by the maidens. Next Hera was led to her bedchamber where she sat on a brocaded boudoir chair before a round, pure-water mirror. Her hair was combed, dressed and ornamented with a hundred tiny orchids. The nymphs pinched her cheeks for color and applied the scarlet juice of crushed cherries to her lips. She was attired in a gown as light as the silver lining of a cloud, and for earring tiny clusters of petite mulberry drops were lovingly placed on each lobe.

Heavenly Mother graciously thanked her nymphs and smiled sweetly until they had all left the room. Once alone, her benevolent grin vanished. She took a last appraising look at herself in the mirror, stood, shouted: "Now! To work!," ran to her chariot, and descended to Zeus' palace. (1)

Another question men ask themselves is who, of men and women, have the most pleasure doing you-know-what? Like most guys, I certainly think we men do, if one can judge from the bodily jolt and moan of a speared bull. Some say that women have and that's the reason they so rarely talk about it, while men, who find it deficient in comparison to women, spend their time in the weight-lifting room discussing little else. Whenever I read a book written by a man who describes how a woman feels sexually, I throw it away because it's simple something no man could possible know, as no woman could possible know the wonderful time we have! No man and no woman, that is, except Tiresias who was both a man and a woman. This is his amazing story, which begins with Hera's eternal complaints about Zeus' infidelities:

"I can no longer put up with your continual complaints," flared Zeus. "All I want is a warm hearth with steaming ambrosia and a stout nectar, my pipe filled, my socks darned, and my favorite chair cleared of dogs. I ask no more than the most common of mortals. I know of mere peasants who live in greater comfort than I.

"But look what I provide you in return. I give you palaces, slaves, rule over the gods, a daily change of robes and sandals, dominions in Heaven and on Earth, plus islands, your own herds and flocks, rivers and lakes, not to speak of countless subjects and a personal Oracle. As for that snide little comment about our bed, don't forget that our honeymoon alone on Samos lasted three-hundred years. Each fortnight you're honored with my presence, and since the pleasures of the boudoir are far greater for women than for men, you enjoy much more satisfaction that I--my flirtations included."

"You're insane. Everyone knows that a man has more pleasure in love than a woman."

"Nonsense. The opposite is true. The proof is that men talk a great deal upon the subject when among themselves to compensate for the lack of the real thing. Whereas women--harlots excluded--keep quiet about it because they are satiated and because if men knew about the enjoyable time women have, they would all want to change their sex. Who would be left then to provide you with your play toys?"

"That's the most outrageous, the sickest thing I've ever heard. But wait. Would you like to put what you've said to a test?" challenged Hera.

"Here you go scheming again. Can't you remain one minute without hatching some new plot?"

"This is no plot and anyway it's you who've asked for it," began defiant Hera. "Listen: One day the mortal seer Teiresias came upon two serpents that were coupling and killed one of them, the female. As always happens in such cases, Teiresias was turned into a woman and spent seven years as such until one day she came upon two other serpents coupling and killed the male, becoming herself a man. He has therefore lived the life of a woman and a man and can tell us who is the receiver of the most pleasure. Would you agree to calling him?"

"I would indeed," accepted Great Father. "Hermes! Hermes!" From the orchard appeared a splendid youth.

"Yes, Father," said tender Hermes in dutiful compliance.

"Go to earth and bring back Teiresias," ordered Zeus.

"That's not necessary, Father," said the young lad. "He's here himself. Athena has turned him into a woman for spying on her in her bath, and she's come to ask you to change her back."

"Ye gods! *You* do it, and then bring him here," commanded quick-tempered Zeus.

"As you see, Husband, if it were so pleasurable to be a woman, why would Teiresias want to be turned back into a man?" concluded self-satisfied Hera.

"That we'll find out right now. Here he comes."

Teiresias, an old man with long, faded hair and an effeminate gait shuffled in. He wore a tattered, purple robe which trained on the floor as he came forward.

"Come here, Teiresias. My wife and I would be grateful if you could shed some light on a rather age-old problem: During ... uh ... the act of love, who has the most pleasure, the man or the woman?"

Hera and Zeus anxiously awaited the answer that was unforthcoming.

"Well, good man, don't leave us in the dark," prodded Zeus.

"Tell my husband what he wishes to know," urged Hera, leaning towards Teiresias, whose quivering lips were on the verge of parting.

"What am I to say?" began frightened Teiresias, looking from the goddess's stern, sagging jowls to Eternal Father's craggy, once-handsome face. "Which of you am I to obey? I'm sure that if I answer that it is men who have the most pleasure, I will receive blows from one of you; while if I answer that it is women, I shall be set upon by the other."

"Have no fear, dear fellow," assured humane Father. "I give you my word that I shall not harm you, and you know that the word of a man if his bond."

"I'm certain one of you will become angry and take revenge upon me," sniffed Teiresias.

"Speak. No one will hurt you," cooed Hera, fingers crossed.

"If I knew which of you was for what..." essayed Teiresias.

"No!" shouted Hera, knowing that Zeus' power would ensure him the vote. "We want only the truth!"

"Would you repeat the question?" quaked Teiresia.

"Of course..." started Zeus.

"It's my turn!" interrupted Hera. "The question is: Who has the most pleasure during sex..."

"Mother!" cried puritanical Father.

"...the *man* or the woman?"

"So as not to offend either of your godlinesses, let me answer with a little verse that you can interpret as you wish."

"Oh, the coward," fumed Hera.

"He's been a woman too long," concluded Zeus. "But say your verse. If it's too obscure we'll take it to one of the Oracles."

"And it'll come back a dozen times less intelligible," said Hera. "But proceed. Tell us your little poem."

Timidly Teiresias began. "If the parts of sexual pleasure he counted as ten, thrice three go to women, only one to men."

"Ha, ha, ha," rejoiced Zeus.

"You mischievous scoundrel," raged Hera, and in her furious anger she blinded Teiresias by casting a baneful spell over him. She then stormed out of the room. (1)

In Greece men were drawn to men for the reason that they could find among themselves that which was lacking elsewhere. It was an impossibility to find fulfillment next to a woman since Greek women were meant to bear children, keep the house and cook. They were uneducated and hadn't even the slightest influence on governing the city-state. Legally, they were eternal minors. There were, happily, exceptions. Pericles' mistress had an opinion concerning politics, but she was a whore and therefore not your everyday Athenian. A huge exception was the Spartans, who literally treated their women like boys, dressing them as such, teaching them arms and educating them so they could take the place of the men when they were off to war. So if Athenian men wanted excitement, they turned to other men. In their lovers and beloveds they found a communion that eclipsed that of family and friends put together because the lover/beloved became their family, was their truest friend, and this even after they had ceased warming each other in bed. When the boy became a man and sought, in his turn, a beloved, his former lover replaced him with a younger model. Through sharing life's experiences and by finding release through mutual lust they were truly one. The exchange of knowledge, the encouragement to face life fearlessly, the determination to never ever disappoint one's beloved and one's lover-- exactly like Leonidas and his 300 at Thermopylae, exactly like the Sacred Band of Thebes—these were the benefits of love between men. Patience, devotion, skill—all the shared experiences that would make of these two an invincible force: this was the secret of a fulfilled life. Education, Xenophon hammered again and again was the key to male love. Mutual education. And sharing, always sharing. The transfer of qualities. The need of bodily contact. Of bodily love. Of shared release. The inescapable truth is this: the Greeks had the wisdom to invent their own gods and to shape their needs and hone their sexuality to their own specifications. The Greeks formed themselves, and then they formed their gods. With modern knowledge perhaps today's men could take things a step further: accept total responsibility for their acts, accept that external superstitions and gods are no longer indispensable. Today we must let our children freely choose their sexuality and place them in an ambience, male and female, that will ensure that choice. We must cease disfiguring them physically with circumcision and disfiguring them mentally with religious hocus-pocus. We must introduce them to the heroes that have fashioned our lives and made progress possible, true heroes not comic-book surrogates. Nature chose my own personal camp for me, sexually, and I'm going to do my best, in this volume and those to come, to prove that I've received a truly proud heritage--a heritage to be truly proud of--thanks to the fabulous men who preferred other men.

SOURCES

(1) From my own book, *TROY*
(2) From my book *ALCIBIADES*
(3) From my book *HADRIAN AND ANTINOUS*
   The major sources for this book are the following:
   <u>Plutarch</u> was born near Delphi around 46 A.D. to a wealthy family. He was married, and a letter to his wife even exists to this day. He had sons, the exact number unknown. He studied mathematics and philosophy in Athens and was known to have visited most of the major Greek sites mentioned in this book, as well as Rome. He personally knew the Emperors Trajan and Hadrian, and became a Roman citizen. He was a high priest at Delphi and his duty consisted of interpreting the auguries of the Pythoness (no mean task). He wrote the *Lives of the Emperors* but alas only two of the lesser emperors survive. Another verily monumental work was *Parallel Lives of Greeks and Romans* of which twenty-three exist. His interest was the destinies of his subjects, how they made their way through the meanders of life. I too have a passionate interest in how men strive their wholes lives for success, only to be crushed, like Alcibiades, like Pericles, at the end. In explanation of his oeuvre Plutarch wrote that what interested him was not history but lives, and the Jekyll/Hyde struggle of virtue versus vice. A small jest, he went on, often reveals more than battles during which thousands

die. His writings on Sparta are nearly all we possess concerning that extraordinary city-state. His major biographies are the *Life of Alexander* and the *Life of Julius Caesar*. Amusingly, Plutarch wrote a scathing review of Herodotus' work in which he stated that the great historian was fanatically biased in favor of the Greeks who could do, according to Herodotus, no wrong.

Thucydides was an Athenian general and historian, contemporary with the events he described. What he wrote was based on what actually happened; there was no extrapolating; no divine intervention on the part of the gods as was the case with Plutarch. An example of this was his observation that birds and animals that ate plague victims died as a result, leading him to conclude that the disease had a natural rather than supernatural cause. His description of the plague has never been equaled, the plague that he himself caught while participating in the Peloponnesian War. He is thought to have died in 411 B.C., the date at which his writing suddenly stops. He admired Pericles and democracy but not the radical form found in Athens.

Herodotus was also contemporary to the events that interest us here. Cicero called him the Father of History, while Plutarch wrote that he was the Father of Lies. His masterpiece is *The Histories*, considered a chef-d'oeuvre, a work that the gods have preserved intact right up to our own day, a divine intervention that would not have surprised a believer like Herodotus (it's also a book I reread every year). Part of his work may have been derived from other sources (what historian's isn't?) and the facts rearranged in an effort to give them dramatic force and please an audience. Much of what he did was based on oral histories, many of which themselves were based on early folk tales, highly suspect, naturally, in all their details. Aristophanes made fun of segments of his work and Thucydides called Herodotus a storyteller. Surprisingly little is known about his own life. For example, he writes lovingly about Samos, leading some to believe that he may have spent his youth there. Born near Ionia, he wrote in that dialect, learning it perhaps on Samos. He was his own best publicist, taking his works to festivals and games, such as the Olympic Games, and reading them to the spectators. As I've said, many people doubt that he actually went where he said he went and saw what he said he saw. But the same was true of Marco Polo who causes disbelief to this day simply because he never mentioned eating noodles in China or seeing the Great Wall or even drinking Chinese tea. But no historian, then as now, can write a book on ancient occurrences without referring to Herodotus' observations. An amusing example of recent discoveries that give credence to Herodotus is this: Herodotus wrote about a kind of giant ant, the size of a fox, living in India, in the desert, that dug up gold. This was ridiculed until the French ethnologist Peissel came upon a marmot living in today's Pakistan that burrows in the sand and has for generations brought wealth to the region by bringing up gold from its burrows. Peissel suggests that the original confusion came from the fact that the Persian word for marmot was similar to the word for mountain ant.

Xenophon, born near Athens in 430 B.C., was a historian and general. His masterpieces are *The Peloponnesian Wars* and *Anabasis*. He loved Sparta and served under Spartan generals during the Persian Wars. Like the Spartans, he believed in oligarchic rule, rule by the few, be they the most intelligent or wealthy or militarily acute. He spent a great deal of time in Persia alongside Cyrus the Younger. Cyrus the Younger was the son of Darius. Cyrus became very friendly with the Spartan Lysander, convinced that Lysander was the only honest man he'd ever met. Lysander helped the Spartans win the Peloponnesus Wars by siding with them. When Darius became ill, Cyrus, astonishingly, turned over his governorship to Lysander, while he went to his father's bedside in Susa. But his brother Artaxerxes, not Cyrus, was named king and Cyrus tried to assassinate him. He failed although he was pardoned, always a mistake from ancient times up to those of the Renaissance. Instead of thanking Artaxerxes for sparing his life, Cyrus the Younger raised an army, among whom were Xenophon's 10,000 and other mercenaries (all of which is the subject of *Anabasis*). Cyrus the Younger met his brother in combat where Cyrus was killed. Cyrus' mother foamed at the mouth at losing her favorite son. According to Plutarch the boy was killed by a soldier named Mithridates who struck him with a blow that felled him from his horse. Cyrus' head was cut off by Artaxerxes' eunuch, Masabates. Cyrus' mother had Mithridates captured and killed by scaphism, the ancient Persian way: The victim was stripped naked and placed between two rowboats that closed one on the other like a walnut, with only the head and arms and legs protruding. He was then feed milk and honey that caused a diarrhea that filled the interior space and attracted insects which would eat and breed in the man's flesh until nothing remained but bone. Later she won Masabates, the eunuch, in a game of dice and had him flayed alive. After Cyrus' death Xenophon and his ten thousand made their way back home, the breathtaking account of which ends his *Anabasis*. The Athenians exiled him when he fought with the Spartans against Athens but the Spartans offered him an estate where he wrote his works. His banishment may have been revoked thanks to his son Gryllus who brilliantly fought and died for Athens. If Xenophon did return to Athens it was a meager consolation as the loss of a son is a man's worst fate.

Of the philosophers, Plato was the major source for this book. Plato's most famous allegory is the Allegory of the Cave. Humans there have no other reality than the shadows they see on the walls. If they looked around they could see what was casting the shadows and by doing so gain additional knowledge. If they left the cave they would discover the sun, analogous to truth. If those who saw the sun reentered the cave and told the others, they would not be believed. There are thusly different levels of reality that only the wisest are able to see; the others remain ignorant. It's basically thanks to Plato and Xenophon that we know what we do about Socrates. Plato's perfect republic is ruled by the best (an aristocracy), headed by a philosopher king who guides his people through wisdom and reason. An inferior form of government, one that comes after an aristocracy, is a timocracy, ruled by the honorable. A timocracy is in the hands of a warrior class. Plato has Sparta in mind, but it's unclear how he could have found this form of government better than, for example, a democracy. The problem may be that we know, in reality, so little about Sparta. Next comes an oligarchy based on wealth, followed by a democracy, rule by just anyone and everyone. This degenerates into a tyranny, meaning a government of oppression, because of the conflict between the rich and the poor in a democracy.

As for the tragedians, we'll begin with <u>Sophocles</u>, author of 123 plays of which 7 remain, notably *Oedipus* and *Antigone*. An Athenian born to a rich family just before the Battle of Marathon, he was a firm supporter of Pericles. He fought alongside Pericles against Samos when the island attempted to become autonomous from Athens. He was elected as a magistrate during the Sicilian Expedition led by Alcibiades, and given for function the goal of finding out why the expedition had ended disastrously. Sophocles was always ready and willing to succumb to the charms of boys. Plutarch tells us that even at age 65 ''he led a handsome boy outside the city walls to have his way with him. He spread the boy's poor himation--a rectangular piece of cloth thrown over the left shoulder that drapes the body--upon the ground. To cover them both he spread his rich cloak. After Sophocles took his pleasure the boy took the cloak and left the himation for Sophocles. This misadventure was eventually known to all.'' He died at 90, some say while reciting a very long tirade from *Antigone* because he hadn't paused to take a breath (apocryphal but charming). Another version has him choking on grapes, and a final one has him dying of happiness after winning the equivalent of our Oscar at a festival. The first of his trilogy--called the Theban plays--is *Oedipus the King*. Here the baby Oedipus--in a plot that goes back to Priam and Paris at the founding of Troy--is handed over to a servant to be killed in order to prevent the accomplishment of an oracle, an oracle stating that he will kill his father and marry his mother. He does both after solving the riddle of the sphinx (which creature becomes four-footed, then two-footed and finally three-footed?). His mother, when she finds out she's been enjoying her own son, commits suicide and Oedipus blinds himself. In *Oedipus at Colonus* Oedipus dies and we learn more about his children Antigone, Polyneices and Eteocles. In *Antigone*

Polyneices is accused of treason and killed. His body is thrown outside the city walls and the king forbids its burial, under pain of death. Antigone does so anyway and, faced with death, she commits suicide, followed by the king's son who was going to wed her, followed by the king's wife who couldn't face losing her precious son. (Wow!)

The father of tragedians was <u>Aeschylus</u>, of whom 7 out of perhaps 90 plays have survived. His gravestone celebrated his heroism during the victory against the Persians at Marathon and *not his plays*, proof of the extraordinary importance of Greek survival against the barbarians (sadly, he lost his brother at Marathon). He is said to have been a deeply religious person, dedicated to Zeus. As a boy he worked in a vineyard until Dionysus visited him in a dream and directed him to write plays. One of his plays supposedly divulged too much about the Eleusinian Mysteries and he was nearly stoned to death by the audience. He had to stand trial but pleaded ignorance. He got off when the judges learned of the death of his brother at Marathon and when Aeschylus showed the wounds he and a second brother had received at Marathon too, the second brother left with but a stump in place of his hand. In one of his later plays, Pericles was part of the chorus. The subjects of his plays often concerned Troy and the Persian Wars, Marathon, Salamis and Xerxes (Xerxes is accused of losing the war due to hubris; his building of the bridge over the Hellespont was a show of arrogance the gods found unacceptable). In *Seven against Thebes* he too tells about Oedipus' two sons. This time the boys agree to become kings of Thebes on alternate years. Naturally, when the time comes for them to change places the king in place refuses, which leads to both boys killing each other. *Agamemnon* is an excellent retelling of the Trojan War, as Agamemnon sails home to be murdered by his wife Clytemnestra. In *The Libation Bearers* Agamemnon's boy Orestes returns home to destroy his father's assassins, Clytemnestra and her lover Aegisthus. In *The Eumenides* (the Kindly Spirits) Orestes is chased by the Furies for having killed his mother. He takes shelter with Apollo who decides, with Athena, to try the boy before a court. The vote is a tie, but Athena, preaching the importance of reason and understanding, acquits him. She then changes the terrible Furies into sweet Eumenides.

<u>Euripides</u> may have written 90 plays of which 18 survive. His approach was a study of the inner lives of his personages, the predecessor, therefore, of Shakespeare. Due to his stance on certain subjects, he thought it best to leave Athens voluntarily rather than suffer an end similar to that of Socrates. An example: ''I would prefer to stand three times to confront my enemies in battle rather than bear a single child!'' He was born on the island of Salamis, of Persian-War fame; in fact he was born on the very day of the battle. His youth was spent in athletics and dance. Due to bad marriages with unfaithful wives, he withdrew to Salamis where he wrote

while contemplating sea and sky. When Sparta defeated Athens in war, it did not destroy the city-state. Plutarch states that this was thanks to one of Euripides' plays, *Electra*, put on for the Spartans in Athens, a play they found so wonderful that they proclaimed that it would be barbarous to destroy a city capable of engendering men of the quality of Euripides. (The real reason was to preserve the city that had twice saved Greece from Persian victory.) Euripides was known for his love of Agathon, a youth praised for his beauty as well as for his culture, and would later become a playwright. Aristophanes mocked Euripides for loving Agathon long after he had left his boyhood behind him. (Remember, not everyone followed boy-love to the letter. The idea of men loving boys until they grew whiskers did not always hold true. Boys grown ''old'' could shave their chins and butts; some men just preferred other men, hairy or not; most men impregnated boys but other men adored being penetrated.) Plato says that Agathon had polished manners, wealth, wisdom and dispensed hospitality with ease and refinement.

<u>Aristophanes</u>, my preferred playwright, is, naturally, the father of comedy. He wrote perhaps 40 plays of which 11 remain. He was feared by all: Plato states that it was his play *The Clouds* the root of the trial that cost Socrates his life. Nearly nothing is known about him other than what he himself revealed in his works. Playwrights were obliged to be conservative because part of each play was funded by a wealthy citizen, an honor for the citizen and a caveat for the author. He was an exponent of make-love-not-war who saw his country go from its wonderful defeat of the Persians to its end at the hands of the Spartans. Along with Alcibiades and Socrates, Aristophanes is featured in Plato's *The Symposium* in which he is gently mocked, proof that he was considered, even by those he poked fun at, as affable. *The Acharnians* highlights the troubles the Athenians went through after the death of Pericles and their defeat at the hands of Sparta. *The Peace* focuses on the Peace of Nicias. *Lysistrata* tells about the plight of women trying to bring about peace in order to prevent the sacrifice of their sons during war, occasioning the world's first sex strike. When Athens lost its freedom to Sparta, Aristophanes stopped writing plays.

Other key sources are: <u>Athenaeus</u> who lived in the times of Marcus Aurelius (meaning we know little about him). His *Deipnosopistae* is a banquet conversation *à la Platon* during which conversations on every possible subject took place, filling fifteen books that have come down to us. <u>Isocrate</u> was a student of Socrates who wrote a speech in the defense of Alcibiades during a trial that took place after his death, but fell on his son who was held responsible for his father's dealings. <u>Cornelius Nepos</u> was a Roman friend of Cicero. Most of what he wrote was lost, so what we know comes through passages of his works in the books of other historians. <u>Andocides</u> was implicated in the Hermes scandal and saved his skin by turning against Alcibiades in a speech that has come down to us called, what else?, *Against Alcibiades*. Lysias was extremely wealthy and contemporary with Alcibiades. He founded a new profession, logographer, which consisted of writing speeches delivered in law courts. One of his speeches was *Against Andocides*, another was *Against Alcibiades*. Diodorus Siculus who lived around 50 B.C. and wrote *Historical Library*, consisting of forty volumes. Pausanias, a Greek historian and geographer, famous for his *Description of Greece*. He was contemporary with Hadrian and Marcus Aurelius. He's noted as being someone interested in everything, careful in his writing and scrupulously honest. Simonides of Ceos was a Greek poet born about 550 B.C. Besides his poems, he added four letters to the Greek alphabet. Bion was a Greek philosopher known for his diatribes, satires and attacks on religion. He lived around 300 B.C. Ovid lived around 10 B.C. A Roman poet especially known for his Metamorphoses, one of the world's most important sources of classical mythology. Polybius was a Greek historian born in Arcadia around 200 B.C. His work describes the rise of the Roman Republic and he is known for his ideas on the separation of powers in government. Aelianus was a Roman author and teacher of rhetoric who spoke and wrote in Greek. Philemon lived to be a hundred but alas only fragments of his works remain. He must have been very popular as he won numerous victories as a poet and playwright. The Greek poet Anacreon was born in 582 B.C. and was known for his drinking songs. Eupolis lived around 430 B.C. An Athenian poet who lived and wrote during the Peloponnesian Wars. Phanocles lived during the time of Alexander the Great. He was the author of a poem on boy-love that described the love of Orpheus for Calais, and his death at the hands of Thracian women. Mimnermus was born in Ionian Smyrna around 630 B.C. He wrote short love poems suitable for performance at drinking parties. Polyenus was a Macedonian known as a rhetorician and for his books on war strategies. Cicero was born in 106 B.C. and murdered by Mark Antony in 43 B.C. Michael Grant said it all when he wrote, ''the influence of Cicero upon the history of European literature and ideas greatly exceeds that of any other prose writer in any language.'' I'll write much more about him in my next book: Volume Two of *HOMOSEXUALITY -Ancient Rome*.

A special mention for Pindar, Theognis and Theocritus. Pindar's great love was Theoxenus of Tenodos about whom he wrote: ''Whosoever, once he has seen the rays flashing from the eyes of Theoxenus, and is not shattered by the waves of desire, has a black heart forged of a cold flame. Like wax of the sacred bees, I melt when I look at the young limbs of boys.'' He lived around 500 B.C. and celebrated the Greek victories against the Persians at Salamis and Plataea. His home in Thebes became a must for his devotees.

I've called on the poet <u>Theognis</u>, born around 550 B.C. His poems consist of maxims and advice as to how to live life. Fortunately, a great deal of his work has come down to us, most of which is dedicated to his beloved, the handsome Cyrnus.

<u>Theocritus</u> was a Sicilian and lived around 270 B.C. I've given a short extract from one of Theocritus' works in the chapter on Socrates, a poem thought so vile that it was put in Latin in Renaissance books. In his 7th Idyll Aratus is passionately in love with a lad. His 12th Idyll refers to Diocles who died saving the life of Philolaus, the boy he loved, and in whose honor kissing contests were held every spring at his tomb. In his 23rd Idyll a lover commits suicide because of unrequited love, warning his beloved that one day he too will burn and weep for a cruel boy. Before hanging himself the lover kissed the doorpost from which he would attach the noose. The boy treated the corpse with disdain and went off to the gymnasium for a swim where a statue of Eros fell on him, coloring the water with his blood. In his 29th Idyll a lover warns his beloved that he too will age and his beauty will lose its freshness. He is therefore advised to show more kindness as ''you will one day be desperate for a beautiful young man's attentions.'' Although lads are often disappointing, it is impossible not to fall madly in love with them. In the 30th Idyll the poet states that when a man grows old he should keep a distance from boys, but in his heart he knows that the only alternative to loving a boy is simply to cease to exist.

And finally here is a list of the books I've read that deal exclusively with Greek boy-love. It does not include the scores I've read that deal with Greek history in general, wars, politics, economics, government, clothing and other nonsexual material. The books below have only served as checks-and-balances to ensure that I've made the fewest possible errors.

Dover K.J. *Greek Homosexuality*, 1978
Halperin David M. *One Hundred Years of Homosexuality*, 1990
Davidson James *The Greeks and Greek Love,* 2007 (The clearest and most
    informative of the three.)

Written somewhere on the Atlantic coast of France, on my tiny sailboat. The year
was 2014

I would be very grateful to have your comments on *HOMOSEXUALITY – The True Lives of Fabulous Men who Preferred other Men*
mbhone@gmail.com

Other books by Michael Hone: TROY; Port Beausoleil; Astorre Manfredi, The most Beautiful Boy of the Italian Renaissance and Hadrian and Antinous, Their Lives and Times; ALCIBIADES – His Role in Athens, Sparta, Persia and Greek Love
(In French: Super Paradis)

Any editor has my permission to publish all or parts of *HOMOSEXUALITY – The True Lives of Fabulous Men who Preferred other Men* as long as I am given credit for the book or extracts taken from the book.   Michael Hone

22494846R00066

Printed in Great Britain
by Amazon